Nitty Gritty Guide

to passing

TExES Technology Applications 242 Exam

Author

Velma Shaw

© Copyright 2019 by (Insert author or publisher name) - All rights reserved.

It is not legal to reproduce, duplicate, or transmit any part of this document in either electronic means or printed format. Recording of this publication is strictly prohibited.

TABLE OF CONTENTS

INTRODUCTION	IV

DOMAIN I

COMPETENCY 001	1
COMPETENCY 002	19
COMPETENCY 003	22

DOMAIN II

COMPETENCY 004	24
COMPETENCY 005	41
COMPETENCY 006	45

DOMAIN III

COMPETENCY 007	52
COMPETENCY 008	58
COMPETENCY 009	62

DOMAIN IV

COMPETENCY 010	64
COMPETENCY 011	70
COMPETENCY 012	78

DOMAIN I-IV QUESTIONS	81
PRACTICE EXAM	100
BIBLIOGRAPHY	125
ACKNOWLEDGMENTS	126

Introduction

Congratulations, on taking the steps to passing the TExES Technology Applications EC-12 (242) exam, you are definitely moving to an exciting and, rewarding career as a Technology Teacher. This book was written to help future educators prepare to pass the TExES 242 content exam by providing the study tools. The book is written based on the comprehensive overview of the TEKS and the competencies within each domain of the Technology Applications EC-12 TExES. The Nitty Gritty Guide is divided into the four domains tested on the TExES 242 exam each of the sections is written as a summative with concise points to outline and reflect the TExES competency objectives manual. There is a practice exam at the end of the book to test your knowledge. Users of Nitty Gritty Guide are advised to study the TEKS as well as, this book but keep in mind more study resources you use gives you a higher chance of passing the exam. The key is preparation to successfully pass and obtain your certification.

Domain I — Technology Applications Core

Competency 001: The Technology Applications teacher knows technology terminology and concepts; the appropriate use of hardware, software and digital files; and how to acquire, analyze and evaluate digital information.

Computer Basics

General Concepts

The language of Computers is binary which consists of 1's and 0's (1 = on, 0 = off). Think of it as a light switch being turn on and off this allow data to pass. The American Standard Code for Information Interchange (ASCII) produces a distinguish code that allows text images to be created and displayed on a computer screen or sent to a printer. There would be no option to be able to work with letters of the alphabet if not for the ASCII code.

Understanding Hardware, Software, and Information

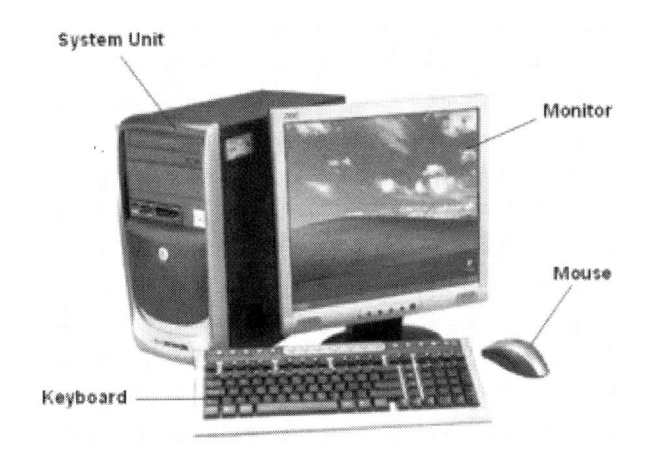

Technology (IT): A computer's hardware is what you can physically see or touch. The software is a computer program that tells the computer hardware how to operate.

Information Technology (IT), is the broad subject related to computers and managing and processing information.

Main Parts of a Personal Computer:

Central Processing Unit (CPU): The computer's brain, the CPU is the computer's main chip. It calculates and processes information, and its speed is measured in Megahertz (MHz) and Gigahertz (GHz).

Hard Disk: The computer's main, long-term storage device.

Common Input Devices:
Mouse: Acts as a handheld pointing device and controls the actions of that blinking item on your computer screen known as a cursor.
Keyboard: Lets you enter information and commands into a computer.
Digital camera: Lets you take pictures and transfer them to a computer.
These devices use a USB, but the Digital Camera uses USB and FireWire

Other Input Devices:
Other input devices include touch pads, AccuPoint® pointing devices, track balls, light pens. scanners, joysticks, and microphones.

Common Output Devices:

Monitors: Resembles and operates a lot like a TV screen. The monitor is only half of what makes text and images appear on the screen. The other half is the graphics card. The monitor plugs into the graphics card in the back of the computer.

Printers: Transfers processed information to printed page. Main types of printers are: InkJet; Laser and color laser; Multifunction; Dot matrix; and Plotter.

Speakers: Allow you to hear the sounds produced by the sound card.

Memory: A computer's temporary storage place, where it gets its work done. There are two main types of memory on your computer:

RAM (random-access memory): Computer's main memory, which is used to process information (example: work with a file). This memory is volatile, which means unsaved data disappears when you shut off the computer.

ROM (read-only memory): Computer's low-level memory, which is used to perform its most basic functions (example: start the computer). This memory is nonvolatile, which means data remains even when you shut off the computer.

Measuring Memory:

Bit: Short for binary digit, a bit is the smallest memory unit. Eight bits equal one byte.

Byte: Short for binary digits eight, one byte equals one character (letter, number, or symbol).

    Kilobyte (K or KB): 1,024 bytes

    Megabyte (M or MB): 1,048,576 bytes

    Gigabyte (G or GB): 1,073,741,824 bytes

    Terabyte (TB): 1,099, 511,627,776 bytes

Computer Performance

CPU Speed: Arguably the single most important factor that determines a computer's performance is the speed of its CPU.

RAM: Generally, the more RAM a computer has the better its performance.

Multitasking: Microsoft Windows can run more than one program at a time. The more programs or tasks being done at a time, the longer it takes to complete each one, and hence a drop-in computer performance.

Software

Graphical User Interface (GUI): Makes computers easier to operate by using pictures and icons to represent files and programs.

An Operating System: Loads automatically and controls just about everything on your computer. Example Windows 10

An Application Program: Helps you accomplish a certain task, such as writing a letter, browsing the Internet, or playing a game.

New Software Versions and Releases: Come out periodically and add new features and improve components of a program. New versions also take advantage of ever-improving technology.

Networks and the Internet

A network comprises two or more computers that have been connected in order to enable them to communicate with each other and share resources and files.

Parts of a network

There are five basic components of a network: clients, servers, channels, interface devices and operating systems.

Servers: Sometimes called host computers, servers are powerful computers that store data or applications and connect to resources that are shared by the users of a network.

Clients: These computers are used by the users of the network to access the servers and shared resources (such as hard disks and printers). These days, it is typical for a client to be a personal computer that the users also use for their own non-network applications.

For example, the personal computers in the School labs are clients, while the computers that store on the H drive: files and all of the web pages are servers.

Channels: Also called the network circuit, the channel is the pathway over which information travels between the different computers (clients and servers) that comprise the network.

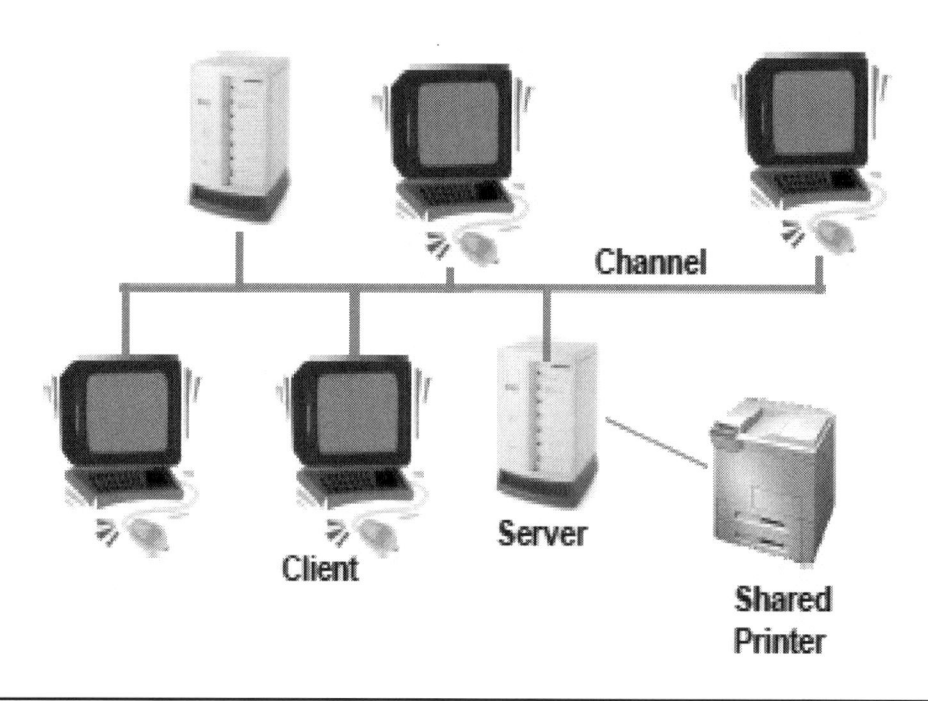

Interface devices: These are hardware devices that connect clients and servers (and sometimes other networks) to the channel. Examples include modems and network interface cards.

Operating systems: The network operating system is the software of the network example Norvell & Microsoft. It serves a similar purpose that the operating system serves in a stand-alone computer.

Understanding network channels

Network channels come in a variety of types, speeds and capabilities. For our purposes, there are four important dimensions of channels:

Transmission medium: This is the actual physical medium of the channel. Computer network channels use either wired or wireless media.

Wired media: Also called guided media and line-based media. In networks that use wireline media, the transmission of information takes place on a wire or cable. The three types of wireline media are twisted-pair wire, coaxial cable and fiber-optic cable. (Try and find examples of each of these media, and their relative speeds).

Wireless media: Also called radiated media. As the name indicates, in networks that use wireless media, there is no physical wire along which information travels; instead, information is transmitted through the air, from one transmission station to the next. Networking examples include radio, cellular, microwave and satellite. Broadcast TV and FM radio use wireless transmission as well (though the underlying engineering is a little different).

Transmission rate or bandwidth: This property of a network channel describes how fast information can be transmitted over the channel. It is measured in bits per second (bps)1. People very commonly use the term bandwidth to mean transmission rate.

Transmission directional capability: The direction in which information can be transmitted over a channel depends on whether the channel is simplex, half-duplex or full-duplex.

Simplex: Information can be transmitted only in one direction

Half-duplex: Information can be transmitted in both directions, but only in one direction at a time

Full-duplex: Information can be transmitted in both directions simultaneously

Signal type: There are two signal types – **analog** and **digital**. It is a little hard to understand the exact difference without discussing a lot of electrical engineering and physics, so will not get that detailed. **What you need to know:**

Analog signals are '**continuous**' (they take on a wide range of values) and **digital** signals are '**discrete**', and binary (take on only two values).

Digital signals are more '**natural**' for computer networks, since, as we know, computers represent all information in binary.

1000 bps = 1 Kbps (kilobit per second); 1000Kbps = 1 Mbps (megabit per second); 1000Mbps = 1Gbps (gigabit per second).

LANs, MANs, WANs and Backbones.

The simplest (and least exact) way of classifying networks is based on the geographic scope of the network. Under this classification, there are four types of networks:

Local Area Networks (LANs): A LAN is confined to a small geographic area. The clients and servers on a LAN are connected to the same channel and are typically in the same building or in neighboring buildings.

Backbone Networks: These are high-bandwidth channels that typically connect LANs with each other and are often referred to as backbones.

Metropolitan Area Networks (MANs) and Wide Area Networks (WANs): A MAN spans a wider geographic area, like a corporate campus or a university, while a WAN is spread over a large geographic area, such as a country or a state.

Networking protocols

Most networks have one feature in common: they transmit information by breaking the original information into a set of messages (called packets), transmitting these packets sequentially, and then reassembling these packets back into the original information. Each packet is a string of bits. However, these packets sometimes must travel a long way, over a bunch of different networks, there are typically lots of computers sending and receiving information over the same network, and the information getting sent can often get altered during transmission (this is called a transmission error). In order to make sure that the original information gets transmitted correctly, efficiently, and to the right place, computer networks use a set of rules, called networking protocols.

By itself, the study of networking protocols could constitute an entire course, this is not necessary just need to know the basics. The primary tasks that protocols are responsible for fall into two categories: network-layer tasks and data-link layer tasks, and the rules associated with each category are called network-layer protocols and data-link layer protocols.

Network-layer protocols: Also called layer-3 protocols. These rules specify how a network does the following three tasks: Packetizing: breaking up the information into packets and reassembling the packets at the receiving end.

Sending information over a computer network

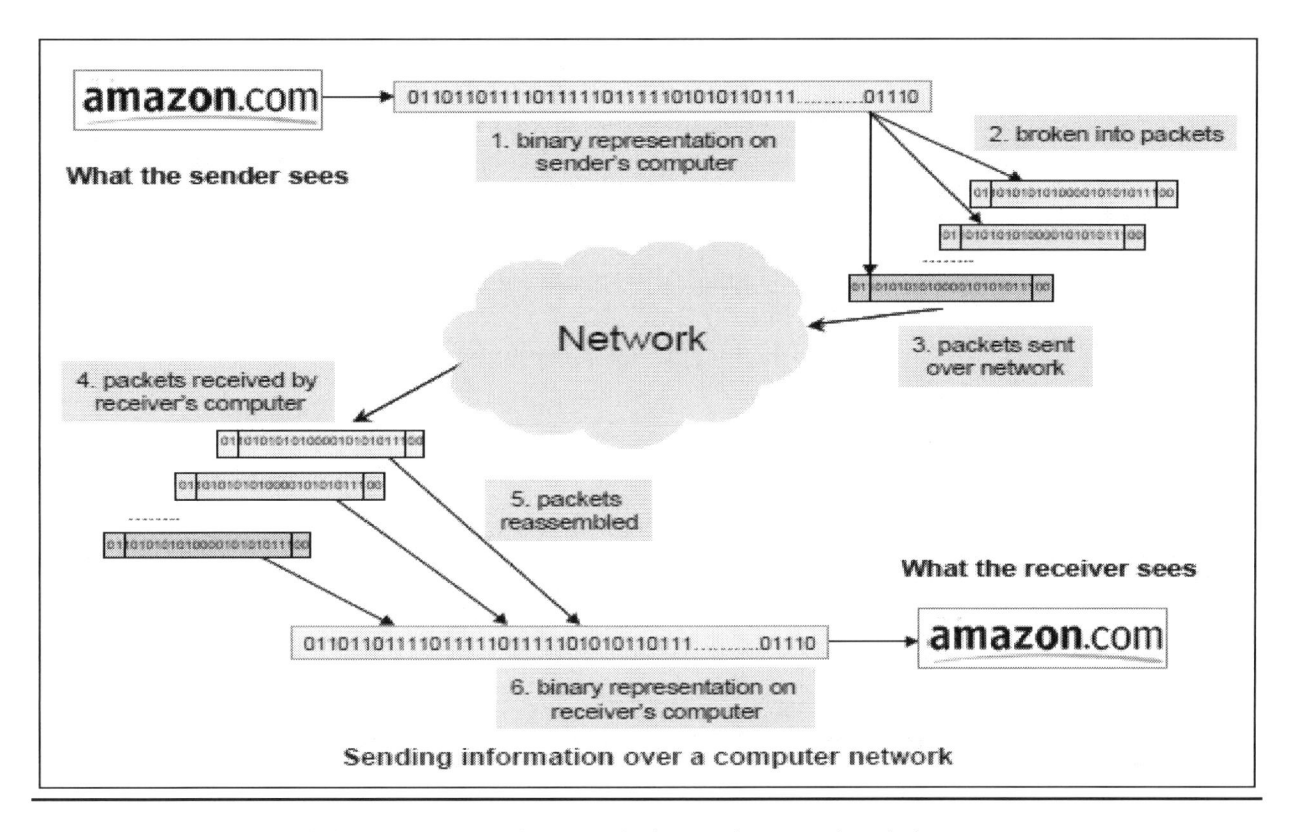

Addressing: Determining which computer and network the packets are headed to.

Routing: Determining the best way for the packets to get to where they are headed.

TCP/IP is a network-layer protocol (and currently the most common one). Another one is IPX/SPX, which was very popular until a few years ago.

Data-link layer protocols: Also called layer-2 protocols. These rules specify how a network does the following three tasks:

•**Delineation:** Figuring out when a message (packet) begins and ends.

•**Error control:** Figuring out when a transmission error has occurred and correcting it.

•**Channel access:** Controlling when a client or server accesses the channel.

There are a wide variety of data-link layer protocols. The most common in organizations and universities is Ethernet which was the first network protocol; another common one is the token ring protocol, developed by IBM. The networks that we connect to from home using a telephone line typically use one of two data link protocols: SLIP or PPP.

Storage Devices

Memory Devices: Memory devices are very useful for sharing or transporting information. They are also useful for backing up your information. A comparison of some of the most common storage devices appears below.

Hard drives: The hard drive is the face of secondary storage in modern computing. Many computers bundle hard drives as internal storage mediums.

Optical media: CDs and DVDs are the most well-known members in the class of optical storage. These mediums are the more efficient successors of the 3.5-inch disk drives. Optical Media refers to discs that are read by laser. CDs& DVD's have a shelf life that last longer than a magnetic hard drive. Optical media have exceptionable read speeds, capacity, and portability.

Drive Secondary storage is named as such because it doesn't have direct access to CPU. As a result, it is considerably slower than primary storage.

A USB flash drive is really another type of Flash Card that plugs into a USB port. USB flash drives range in sizes from 16 MB to 512 MB.

File Formats

The software in which a file is created usually uses a default format when the file is saved. This is indicated by the file name suffix (e.g., **.PDF** for portable document format). However, most software allows authors to select from a variety of formats when they save a file. For example, Microsoft Word allows the author to select document [**DOC**], Rich Text Format [**RTF**], or text [**TXT**], as well as other format options. Some software, such as Adobe Acrobat, is designed to convert files from one format to another. The format you choose will affect your long-term records management abilities.

KEY CONCEPTS

When considering the file format options available it is important to be familiar with the following concepts:

Proprietary, Non-Proprietary, Open Source, and Open Standard File Formats

Proprietary formats. Proprietary file formats are controlled and supported by just one software developer. Microsoft Word (.DOC) format is on example.

Non-proprietary formats. These formats are supported by more than one developer and can be accessed with different software systems. eXtensible Markup Language (XML) is a popular non-proprietary format for government records.

Open Source formats. In general, open source refers to any program whose source code is made available for use or modification as users or other developers see fit. Open source formats are published publicly available specifications for storing data which are often maintained by a standards organization. Open formats can be used by proprietary and open source software alike.

Open Standard formats. Open standard software formats are created using publicly available specifications (open source formats). Although software source codes remain proprietary, the availability of the standard increases compatibility by allowing other developers to create hardware and software solutions that interact with, or substitute for, other software.

When choosing a file format to use for an electronic records management purposes, it is important to understand how proprietary, non-proprietary, open formats, and open standards may affect the accessibility and accountability of the records over the long term.

File Types and their Associated Formats

Text files. Text files are most often created in word processing software programs. Common file formats for text files include:

Proprietary formats, such as Microsoft Word files, which carry the extension of the software in which they were created.

RTF or Rich Text Format files are supported by a variety of applications and saved with formatting instructions (such as page layout).

Portable Document Format (PDF) files, which contain an image of the page, including text and graphics. PDF files are widely used for read-only file sharing. Adobe Acrobat is, by far, the most popular PDF file application, although others are available.

Portable Document Format (PDF/A) files. PDF/A, as standard file format for long-term archiving of electronic documents, is a subset of PDF. Files are 100% self-contained, and do not rely on outside sources for document information. ISO standard: ISO 19005-1:2005.

Graphics files. Graphics files store an image (e.g., photograph, drawing) and are divided into two basic types; vector-based and raster-based.

Vector-based files store an image as mathematical formulas. Vector image programs use this mathematical formula to display and scale the image without distortion. Common types of vector-based file formats include: SVG, EPS.

Drawing Interchange Format (DXF) files, which are widely used in computer-aided design software programs, such as those used by engineers and architects.

Encapsulated PostScript (EPS) files, which are widely used in desktop publishing software programs.

Computer Graphics Metafile (CGM) files, which are widely used in many image-oriented software programs (e.g., Photoshop) and offer a high degree of durability.

Shapefiles (SHP), ESRI GIS applications use vector coordinates to store non-topological geometry and attribute information for features.

Raster-based files store the image as a collection of pixels. Raster graphics are also referred to as bitmapped images. Raster graphics cannot be scaled without distortion. Common types of raster-based file formats include:

Bitmap (BMP) files are relatively low-quality files used most often in word processing applications. Uncompressed.

Tagged Image File Format (TIFF) files are usable with many different software programs and are often the format of choice for a high-quality master image. Uncompressed or lossless compression.

Joint Photographic Experts Group (JPEG) files are very common format for digital photography. JPEGs are also the preferred format for Internet delivery and file sharing of photographs. Lossy compression.

Joint Photographic Experts Group (JPEG2000). An evolving format with multiple compression techniques based on wavelet technology. Lossless compression.

Graphics Interchange Format (GIF) files were widely used on the Internet for graphics and logos with areas of solid color. Due to color limitations, photographs are not accurately represented with this format. GIF can also be used for low resolution animations. (PNG has improved on the color limitations of GIF.) Lossless compression.

Portable Network Graphic (PNG) files, designed to replace GIF, are patent and license free and produce higher quality files than GIF. PNG format is preferred for images that contain text or line art, especially on the Internet. Lossless compression.

Data files. Data files are created in database software programs and are therefore often represented proprietary formats. Data files are divided into fields and tables that contain discrete elements of information. The software builds the relationships between these discrete elements. For example, a customer service database may contain customer name, address, and billing history fields. These fields may be organized into separate tables (e.g., one table for all customer name fields).

Spreadsheet files. Spreadsheet files store the value of the numbers in their cells, as well as the relationships of those numbers. For example, one cell may contain the formula that sums two other cells. Like data files, spreadsheet files are most often in the proprietary format of the software program in which they were created. Data can be shared between different spreadsheet programs by saving individual spreadsheets as a text file in the Data Interchange Format (DIF), however the value and relationship of the numbers may be lost.

Video and audio files. These files contain moving images (e.g., digitized video, animation) and sound data. They are most often created and viewed in proprietary software programs and stored in proprietary formats. Common files formats in use include QuickTime (.MOV), Windows Media Video (.WMV), and Motion Picture Experts Group (MPEG) formats (.MP3); others include .AVI and .WAV files.

Markup languages. Markup languages, also called markup formats, contain embedded instructions for displaying or understanding the content of the file. They provide the means to transmit and share information over the web. The following markup language file formats are supported by the World Wide Web Consortium (W3C) as standards

Standard Generalized Markup Language (SGML), a common markup language used in government offices worldwide, is an international standard. HTML and XML are derived from SGML.

Hypertext Markup Language (HTML) is used to display most of the information on the World Wide Web. Because presentation is combined with content through the use of pre-defined tags, HTML is simple to use but limited in scope. Other markup languages such as XHTML and XML offer greater flexibility.

eXtensible Markup Language (XML) is a relatively simple language based on SGML that is gaining popularity for managing and sharing information. XML provides even greater flexibility and control than XHTML while avoiding the complexities associated with SGML.

eXtensible Hypertext Markup Language (XHTML) combines the flexibility found in XML with the ease of use associated with HTML. Strict XHTML rules improve consistency and provide the ability to create your own markup tags. Because they share similar rules, converting XHTML into XML is easier that converting HTML into XML.

Table 1: Common File Formats

File Format Type	Common Formats	Sample Files	Description
Text	PDF, RTF, TXT, DOC	Letters, reports, memos, e-mail messages saved as text	Created or saved as text (may include graphics)
Vector graphics	DXF, EPS, CGM, SHP	Architectural plans, complex illustrations, GIS	Store the image as geometric shapes in a mathematical formula for undistorted scaling
Raster graphics	TIFF, BMP, GIF, JPEG, PNG	Web page graphics, simple illustrations, photographs	Store the image as a collection of pixels which cannot be scaled without distortion
Data file	Proprietary to software program	Human resources files, mailing lists	Created in database software programs
Spreadsheet file	Proprietary to software program, DIF	Financial analyses, statistical calculations	Store numerical values and calculations
Video and audio files	QuickTime (MOV), MPEG, Real Networks (RM), WMV, WAV, MP3, AVI	Short video to be shown on a web site	Contain moving images and sound
Markup languages	SGML, HTML, XHXML, XML	Text and graphics to be displayed on a web site	Contain embedded instructions for displaying and understanding the content of a file or multiple files

Preservation: Conversion and Migration

Preserving files must be verified often because file formats change and may not be supported anymore. When formats are no longer supported, a decision is made to convert and/or migrate the file formats. If the file is converted the format must be changed perhaps to a software-independent format. If the files are migrated, it should be moved another platform or storage medium, without changing the file format. However, a possibility to convert the files in order to migrate them to ensure that they remain accessible. For example, if a file is migrated from an Apple operating system to a Microsoft Windows operating system, this file may need to be converted to a file format that is accessible in a Windows operating system (e.g., RTF, Word).

Three basic types of loss (Data, Appearance, Relationship) when converting or migrating files. The amount and type of loss needs to be analyzed to determine the best course of action. **The three types of loss are:**

Data: If data is loss or if it becomes corrupted, the content of the record is lost. Metadata may also be altered or lost.

Appearance: If you convert all word processing documents to RTF, there is a risk of losing the structure of the record as well as, a loss of the page layout.

Relationships: Another risk is the loss of the relationships of the data within the file or between files (e.g., spreadsheet cell formulas, database file fields).

Compression

As part of your records management strategy, you may choose to compress your files. A few of the pros and cons are summarized below.

Table 2: Pros and Cons of File Compression

Pros	Cons
Saves storage space	May result in data loss
More quickly and easily transmittable	Introduces an additional layer of software dependency (the compression software)

Compressing files results in a smaller file size, which reduces the amount of storage space needed. However, to create a smaller file size, information is often removed from the file. For example, when an image file is compressed, pixels that the software determines will not be missed are removed, relying on the human eye to fill in the absent details. When an audio file is compressed, sounds often unnoticeable to the human ear are removed, resulting in a smaller file size that, to most people, sounds the same as the uncompressed file. Compression options vary in their degree of data loss. Some are intentionally "lossy," such as the ones described above while others are designed to be "lossless." Lossless compression results in a smaller file size but allows for exact reconstruction of the original file from the compressed data, unlike lossy compression which only approximates the original data.

E-book Format Files

    PC or Mac — **EPUB or PDF**

    iPad, iPhone, and iPod Touch — **EPUB or PDF**

    Kindle and Kindle Fire — **MOBI or PDF**

    Android — **EPUB**

    NOOK, NOOK Color and NOOK Tablet — **EPUB**

    Sony Reader and Other eReaders — **EPUB**

Search Strategy Using Boolean Operators

Boolean operators are used in computer database searching to connect research concepts. Boolean operators generally use only three words: and, or, and not. Here is how they work.

"AND" narrows the search topic because both concepts must be in each record.

If we specify chocolate and cake and ice cream, the database will give us a list of sources in which all three concepts are mentioned.

"OR" broadens the search topic because all records containing one or both terms are included. If you need to broaden your topic, add synonyms or other phrases to the search strategy.

"NOT" eliminates unrelated records containing the concept.

Concept 1 not Concept 2-chocolate cake not ice cream

Once you have set up a search strategy, you're ready to take the next step, searching and locating research information on the research topic.

Digital Citizenship is defined as someone who navigates the possibilities and pitfalls of the digital world safely, responsibly, and respectfully.

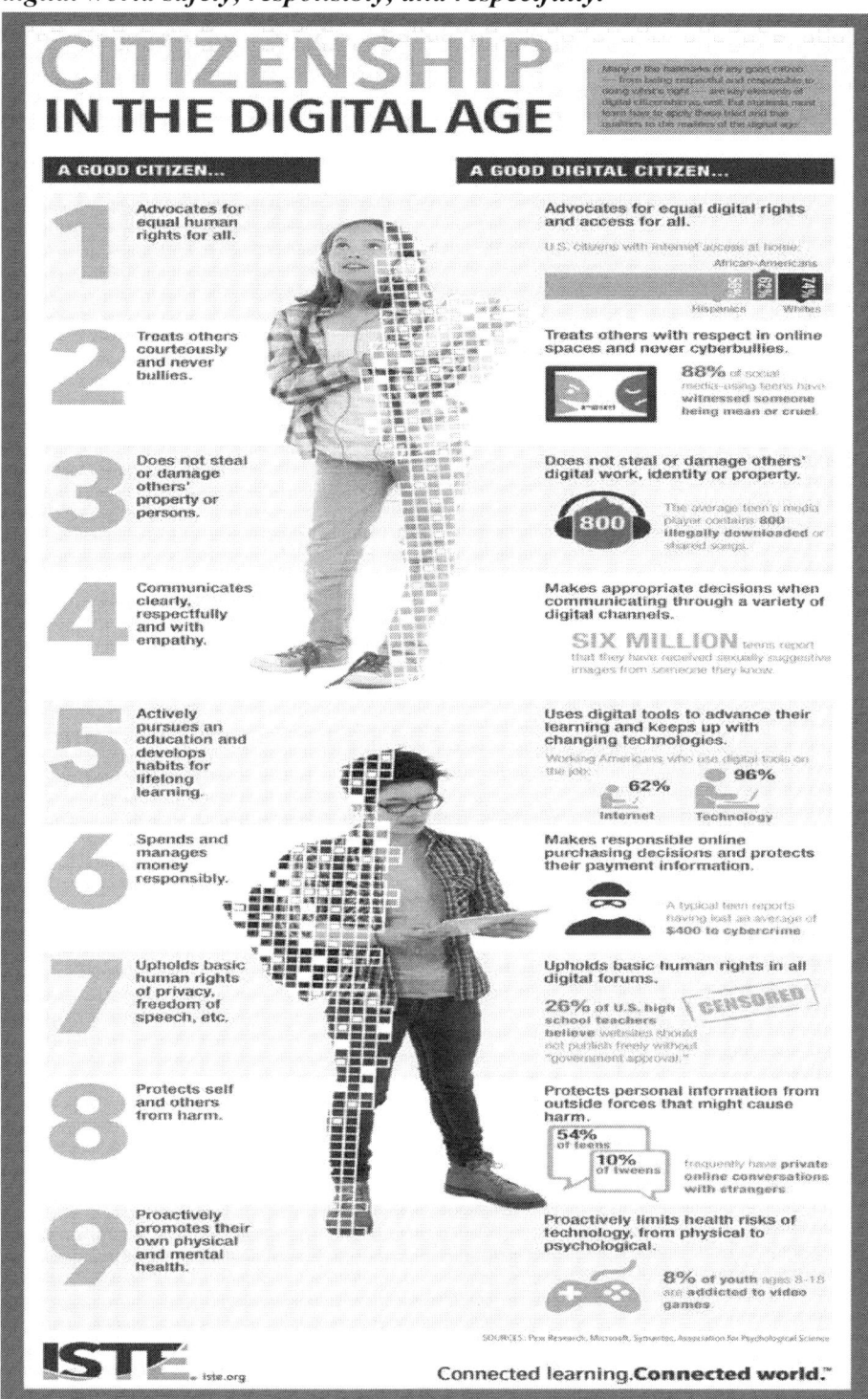

Copyright, fair use policies, and when it is a smart idea to get authorization from parents/guardians to use photographs and recordings of minors are significant issues.

There is a great deal of ethical contemplation when delivering materials for the web or printed school productions, for example, newspapers and yearbooks. Unfortunately, not all school districts have clear rules.

Some school administrators mistakenly interpret **Family Educational Rights and Privacy (FERPA laws)** to imply that student pictures can't be used in school records and productions without the consent of parents or guardians. As a general rule, **FERPA** laws show that school district employees can't release or publish students information or photographs to the general public without the consent of the parents, in any case, most school yearbooks, school TV projects and school newspapers are created by students, so keep in mind that projects that are produced by students do not fall under the **FERPA** laws.

The First Amendment of the Constitution ensures that photos taken in public places, for example, school cafeterias, school events, school grounds, school corridors, and in libraries, did not require consent to be used. When taking photographs at a school sports game such as, football, envision how troublesome it is getting a permission document for each student in the stand.

Copyright occurs when a newspaper is distributed, TV program or a YouTube video is posted online. Because you don't see the copyright image does not mean the work is "public domain". An individual isn't required to register a publication with the Copyright Office.

The copyright holder has the exclusive rights to reproduce and distribute their work. and, allow authorization to others to use the work.

Commercial music should never be incorporated into a blog, podcast without the consent of the copyright holder. digital recording posted on the Internet without authorization from the duplicate right holder.

If the copyrighted work is used for nonprofit or educational purposes than fair use limits the copyright holder's exclusive rights. Such as, if a teacher copies a web page photo or use a page out of a book for a class presentation during a semester than this is acceptable. This is not acceptable if the teacher uses the copy material continuously yearly. Many teachers follow the one semester rule, which means use for one semester only. Additionally, utilizing copyright pictures on a school or classroom website, is less inclined to be viewed as fair use.

Music being used for a student or teacher presentation should not be used more than 30 seconds. Video clips should not be longer than three minutes and only five images from an artist. Copyrighted material for the purpose of criticism, comment, and parody extends to fair use if only using small number of items.

Most schools understand that students should not be left unattended on the Internet and adopt adequate use approaches. **The National Education Association** proposes that a compelling AUP ought to contain: 1) a prelude or objective of why the AUP has been created; 2) meanings of terms showing up; 3) a strategy / policy statement outlining when students may use the Internet; 4) satisfactory uses documented; 5) unacceptable uses laid out; 6) how infringement of the AUP will be handled.

Synopsis: Do not use copyright material for commercial purposes without consent. Teachers may have fair use to copyright material, if they are not creating and selling an item with copyright material included, and, when they use copyright material, they are restricting the use of the materials to short music cuts, video clips, or content entries (10 percent or less).

Creative Commons was established in 2002 this allowed the chance for individuals, for example, artists, musicians, craftsmen, performers and so on to distribute their work on an open content platform. CC is the acronym for Creative Commons it is by a wide margin the most utilized licensing for Open Content. Its prevalence and boundless use imply CC would nowadays be able to be viewed as accepted as the standard for Open Content licensing. **There are a few creative normal licenses:**

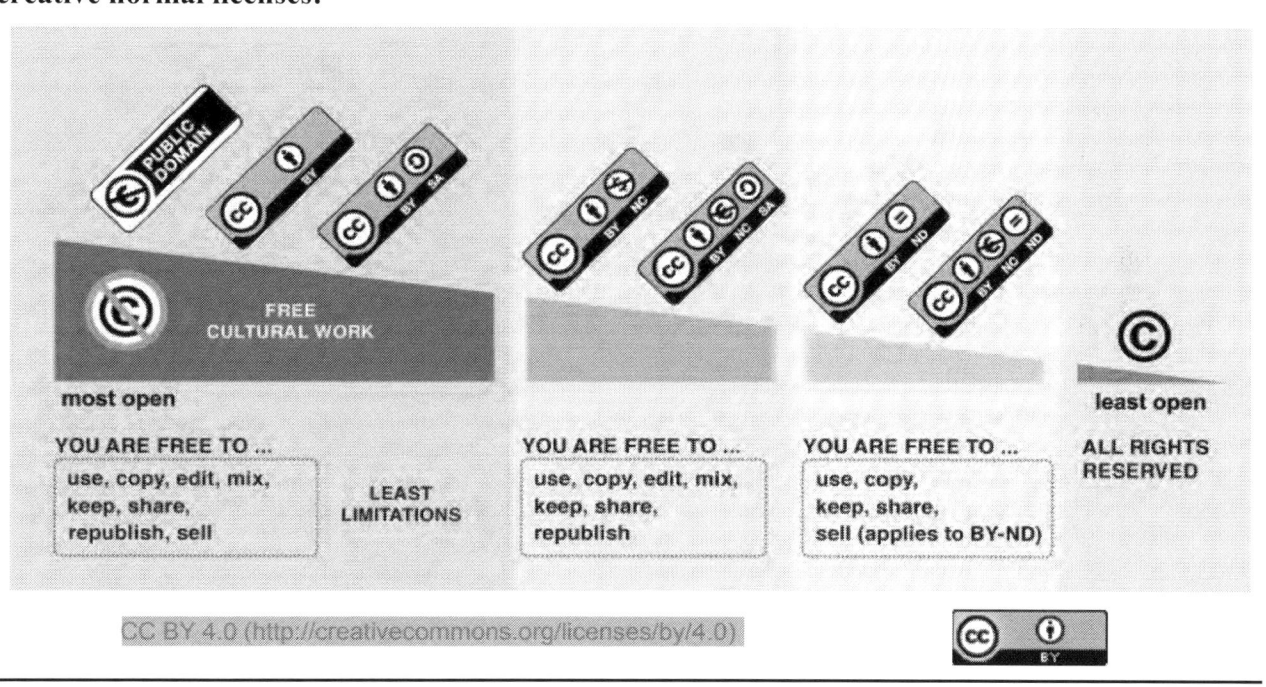

	most open			least open
	YOU ARE FREE TO ...	YOU ARE FREE TO ...	YOU ARE FREE TO ...	ALL RIGHTS RESERVED
	use, copy, edit, mix, keep, share, republish, sell	use, copy, edit, mix, keep, share, republish	use, copy, keep, share, sell (applies to BY-ND)	
		LEAST LIMITATIONS		

CC BY 4.0 (http://creativecommons.org/licenses/by/4.0)

17

Ways to Be Safe Online

1. Keep Personal Information Professional and Limited

2. Keep Your Privacy Settings On

3. Practice Safe Browsing

4. Make Sure Your Internet Connection is Secure

5. Be Careful What You Download

6. Choose Strong Passwords.

7. Make Online Purchases from Secure Sites

8. Be Careful What You Post

9. Be Careful Who You Meet Online

10. Keep Your Antivirus Program Up to Date

Competency 002: The Technology Applications teacher knows how to use technology tools to solve problems, evaluate results and communicate information in a variety of formats for diverse audiences.

Analytic Graphics are also called business graphics; graphical forms that make numeric data easier to analyze than it is when organized as rows/columns of numbers. The principal examples of analytical graphics are bar charts, line graphs/pie charts.

Cell is place where a row/a column intersect in a spreadsheet worksheet; its position is called a cell reference or a cell address. A cell is the smallest working unit in a spreadsheet. Data/formulas are entered "Cells ". "Cell " addresses provide location references for worksheet users.

CAD Computer Aided Draft -- Programs intended for the design of products, structures, civil engineering drawings/maps. CAD programs, which are available for microcomputers, help architects design buildings and workspaces and help engineers design cars, planes, electronic devices, roadways, bridges/subdivisions. while similar to drawing programs, CAD" programs provide precise dimensioning/positioning of the elements being drawn, so they can be transferred later to computer-aided manufacturing programs.

Database--Collection of interrelated files in a computer system. these computer-based files are organized according to their common elements, so that they can be retrieved easily. Many businesses & organizations build databases to help them keep track of and or manage their efforts, in addition, online database services put enormous resources at the user's disposal.

Database Software also called database manager or database management system **(DBMS)**; application software that sets up/controls the structure of a database/access to the data. Database software allows users to organize/manage huge amount of data.

Desktop Publishing---Application software/hardware system that involves mixing text/graphics to produce high-quality output for commercial printing. using a microcomputer/mouse, scanner, digital cameras, laser or ink-jet printer/DTP software. Desktop Publishing DPT has reduced the number of steps, the time/the money required to produce professional looking printed projects.

Device Drivers---Specialized software programs-usually components of system software- that allows input/output devices to communicate with the rest of the computer system Device Drivers are needed so that the computer's operating system can recognized/run peripheral hardware.

Formulas --- in a spreadsheet, instructions for calculations entered into designated cells. When spreadsheet users change data in one cell, all the cells linked to it by formulas automatically recalculate their values.

Functions----In a spreadsheet, built-in formulas that perform common calculations. Functions after the values have been entered into the worksheet, formulas/functions can be used to calculate outcomes.

$ dollar ----- when a formula is copied to another row with a dollar sign in front of the column letter, the cell address updates only by the row number. The dollar sign acts as an anchor to the row number or column letter that it is in front of when you copy the formula or cell address to another cell.

PDF---File format developed by Adobe systems, pdf captures text, graphic and formatting information from a variety of applications on different platforms making it possible to send documents/have them appear on the recipient's monitor (or printer) as they were intended to be viewed. A properly prepared PDF file maintains the original fonts (type styles/type sizes), images, colors and graphics, as well as the exact layout of the file. A PDF file can be shared, viewed/printed by anyone using the free downloadable Adobe Reader software. PDF can also be used on mobile devices. With the complete Adobe Acrobat suite, users can also edit PDF files.

Program Management Software PM---Program used to plan/schedule the people, costs and resources required to complete a project on time. Program Management Software increases the ease/speed of planning/managing complex projects.

Public Domain Software ----Software, often available on the internet, that is not protected by copyright/thus may be duplicated by anyone at will.

Range----A group of adjacent cells in a spreadsheet for example: A1 to A5. Ranges help sort data for calculations or reports.

Recalculation----The process of recomputing values in a spreadsheet, either as an ongoing process as data is entered or afterward, with the press of a key. This simple feature, the hours of mind-numbing work required to manually rework paper spreadsheets have become a thing of the past.

Rollover----Icon feature, also called a tooltip, in which a small text box explaining the icon's function appears when you roll the mouse pointer over the icon. A rollover may also produce an animated graphic.

Software license----Contract by which users agree not to make copies of software to give away or resell.

Workbook---Application software that allows users to create tablets and financial schedules by entering data/formulas into rows and columns arranged as a grid on a worksheet display screen.

System Software----The software that runs at the most basic level of your computer to perform essential operating tasks/enables the application software to run. The most important component of system software is the operating system, the master control program that runs the computer.

Template---In word processing, a preformatted document that provides basic tools for shaping a final document- the text, layout/style for a letter. Template make it very easy for users to prepare professional looking documents, because most of the preparatory formatting is done.

Utilities-Also known as service programs; system software components that perform tasks related to the control, allocation/maintenance of computer resources. Utilities enhance existing functions or provide services not supplied by other system software programs. Most computers come with built-in utilities as part of the system software; they usually include backup, data recovery, virus protection, data compression/file defragmentation, along with disk cleanup.

Value---A number or date entered in a spreadsheet cell.

Web Apps--Software that runs on a remote internet server rather than on a person's own personal computer.

Web Page Design, Authoring Software used to create web pages with sophisticated multimedia features.

Presentation Software example Microsoft PowerPoint. Software that uses graphics, animation, sound/data or information to make visual presentations.

The most important part of the student's presentation is its content; multimedia projects in education are all about showing the depth of knowledge acquired. The second most important aspect is the effectiveness of the presentation and the skill of the presenters. The presentation should be evaluated on what the students learned and how they presented/communicated it, not how well they can use the special effects or the software.

Communicating information in a variety of formats using technology this is the most flexible component because it can be personalized for students such as, work with what you got, get imaginative with text, use tech to benefit learners on a social-emotional level, remove social barriers and stay inclusive.

Competency 003: The Technology Applications teacher knows how to plan, organize, deliver and evaluate instruction that effectively utilizes current technology for teaching the Technology Applications Texas Essential Knowledge and Skills (TEKS) for all students.

Teaching Strategies for diverse learners

Active learning strategies put your students at the center of the learning process, enriching the classroom experience and boosting engagement.

As opposed to traditional learning activities, experiential learning activities build knowledge and skills through direct experience.

Project-based learning uses an open-ended approach in which students work alone or collectively to produce an engaging, intricate curriculum-related questions or challenges.

Inquiry-based learning is subdivided into four categories, all of which promote the importance of your students' development of questions, ideas and analyses.

Adaptive learning focuses on changing — or "adapting" — learning content for students on an individual basis, particularly with the help of technology.

Formative assessment

The goal of formative assessment is to monitor student learning to provide ongoing feedback that can be used by instructors to improve their teaching and by students to improve their learning. **More specifically, formative assessments:**

Help students identify their strengths and weaknesses and target areas that need work

Help faculty recognize where students are struggling and address problems immediately

Formative assessments are generally low stakes, which means that they have low or no point value. **Examples of formative assessments include asking students to:**

> **Draw a concept map in class to represent their understanding of a topic**
>
> **Submit one or two sentences identifying the main point of a lecture**
>
> **Turn in a research proposal for early feedback**

Summative assessment

The goal of summative assessment is to evaluate student learning at the end of an instructional unit by comparing it against some standard or benchmark.

Summative assessments are often high stakes, which means that they have a high point value. Examples of summative assessments include:

> **a midterm exam**
>
> **a final project**
>
> **a paper**
>
> **a senior recital**

Information from summative assessments can be used formatively when students or faculty use it to guide their efforts and activities in subsequent courses.

The Americans With Disabilities Act (ADA) encourages teachers to assist students adapt to the classroom. This is always advisable for visually impaired students should be placed near the front of the class.

Teaching strategies such as, cooperative learning can be used to include students by encouraging student to interact, explore, and discover this strategy is more effective than a teacher lecturing only in a classroom. Students are placed in a mixed (heterogeneous)-ability (various learning) groups and guided through activities by the Teacher.

Cooperative groups: 1) face each other; 2) are no more than five students; 3) mix groups academically, socially, and by gender; 4) rotate groups occasionally; 5) provide specific instructions; 6) start with doable projects; and, 7) have specific roles for each student.

Teaching Strategy tool is KWHL

A KWHL chart should be used before, during, and after a student reads about a new topic. Filling out this chart prepares a student for learning about a topic, helps in reviewing what has been learned about the material, gives help in obtaining more information, and readies the student to write about what they've learned.

> K stands for what you already KNOW about the subject.
>
> W stands for what you WANT to learn.
>
> H stands for figuring out HOW you can learn more about the topic.
>
> L stands for what you LEARN as you read.

Domain II — Digital Art and Animation

Competency 004: The Technology Applications teacher demonstrates knowledge of the principles and elements of design and their application to digital art and animation.

What is Digital Art?

In its broadest extant sense, "digital art" refers to art that relies on computer-based digital encoding, or on the electronic storage and processing of information in different formats—text, numbers, images, sounds—in a common binary code. The ways in which art-making can incorporate computer-based digital encoding are extremely diverse. A digital photograph may be the product of a manipulated sample of visual information captured with a digital camera from a "live" scene or captured with a scanner from a traditional celluloid photograph. Music can be recorded and then manipulated digitally or created digitally with specialized computer software. And a movie is now the product of an extremely complex sequence of choices between analog and digital processes at the stages of image and sound capture or composition, image and sound editing, color correction or sound mastering, special effects production, and display or projection.

In the digital environment we don't have wood, charcoal, or paint. Everything is the same—just a combination of 0's and 1's translated to a visual form on the screen. These 0's and 1's can simulate any medium you can imagine. Just like a proper piece of software can turn your computer into a violin, a piano, or drums, another one can turn it into a canvas and a palette full of various paints. The instruments are not real, but the sounds are, and so is the image.

Although digital art is not bound by the rules of traditional art, it often simulates it to give the user something familiar and to make the whole process more intuitive for the artist. Early digital painting programs were based on coloring the pixels with a mouse, but today they offer much more: the digital paint blends naturally, can be mixed, and is applied with a special stylus on a graphics tablet.

An example of ASCII art is:

```
 (\_/)
(='.'=)
(")^(")
```

Forms of Digital Visual Arts

Digital Drawing

The stylus can only have one shape, and this shape is usually like a pencil or a marker.

Digital Sculpting

Sculpting in the digital environment is based on creating a 3D image—one that can be rotated and viewed from many angles.

Digital Photography

The artist uses a digital or conventional camera. The photographs are digitized and translated to the computer environment where the artist uses image editing and special effects software to perform darkroom type manipulations.

Photopainting

This combines the disciplines of photography and painting. The artist uses image editing and paint software to go beyond dark room techniques to add further expression to the image.

Digital Collage

This is a technique of combining many images from varying sources into one image. This is most commonly achieved using layering techniques in image editing and paint software.

2D Digital Painting

The artist creates 2D images totally in the computer virtual environment with the use of painting tools that emulate natural media styles. Sometimes referred to as "Natural Media".

3D Digital Painting

The artist uses3D modeling and rendering software to essentially sculpt in virtual space. This method also makes use of all the other methods.

Vector Drawing

The artist uses vector drawing software and creates the image totally in the virtual environment. This makes use of shapes which are outlined and can be filled with various colors and patterns. This tends to produce a harder edged or graphic look.

Algorithmic / Fractals

This is art produced exclusively by mathematical manipulations. This is the so-called "computer generated" art. The art here lies in the invention of the mathematical formulas themselves and the way the programs are written to take advantage of the display capabilities of the hardware. The art also lies in the creative intentions and subsequent selections of the artist/mathematician.

Integrated Art

This is the "mixed media "of the digital art world. Artists combine any number of the techniques to achieve unique results. The digital environment is much less restricted than conventional mediums in this type of integration and manipulation.

Animation

Because the screen is displaying the image continuously, nothing stops it from displaying a slightly different image every fraction of a second to create the illusion of movement. Such a moving image can be created by drawing each frame by hand, or by copying and editing the previous frame. Both 2D and 3D art can get animated.

Elements of art

Line Shape

A continuous mark made on a surface or in space. Can be defined as the path of a moving point. Lines can be made with a variety of tools including brushes, pencils and pens. In sculptural work lines can be made with wire, steel, wood or any other material that is used to create a narrow mark in space. Common words or adjectives for describing lines are straight, curvy, horizontal, vertical, diagonal, zigzag, bold, light and angular LINE

Contour Lines are lines that describe an edge.

Contour and Cross Contour Lines are lines that describe surfaces, texture, form and volume.

Organic vs. Geometric Lines Organic lines are lines that imitate the lines and shapes found in nature. Geometric lines are lines with hard edges and angles that replicate lines found in manmade objects or geometry. Adjectives: Smooth Curved Flowing Rounded Adjectives: Angular Straight Sharp Hard

Line Weight Line weight refers to the thickness or thinness of a line. It can be used to give a feeling or tension and weight or emphasis. The weight of a line may also be used to create a sense of motion or depth.

Shape is an enclosed space. Shapes are created by an enclosed line or the difference between one or more elements of art; for example, value, color, or texture. Shape is measured by height and width only. Shapes may be positive or negative, organic/biomorphic, or geometric. They are also used in two- or three- dimensional work. Shape

Organic and Geometric Shapes Like organic lines, Organic Shapes mimic shapes found in nature. Geometric Shapes are also like geometric lines, they mimic man made shapes and generally have corners and flat sides.

2-D and 3-D Shapes Two-Dimensional Shapes are shapes drawn on a flat surface. Three-Dimensional Shapes are shapes created in real or three-dimensional space.

Positive and Negative Shapes Positive Shapes exist in positive space. They are usually objects or things that occupy the foreground of a two-dimensional work of art or they are the parts of a three- dimensional sculpture. Negative Shapes are the shapes that exist between positive shapes or spaces. These shapes become the background. Negative shapes mimic the positive shapes and are as important to creating a successful work of art as the positive shapes.

Space is the area between or within shapes or forms. It can be Space is the area between or within shapes or forms. It can be manipulated to create the illusion of depth in a two dimensional manipulated to create the illusion of depth in a two-dimensional work of art. Space can be positive or negative. The area within the work of art. Space can be positive or negative. The area within the objects of a composition is objects of a composition is positive space positive space. The area surrounding the. The area surrounding the primary objects of a composition is primary objects of a composition is negative space negative space.

Figure Ground Relationship. The relationship between positive and negative shapes or spaces in a composition is known as the figure ground relationship. Figure is the name given to the objects in a composition we see as positive space and ground refers to the shapes we see as negative space. In a composition with a reversible figure ground relationship, like the image to the right, the shapes shown could be positive or negative depending on how you look at it.

Two and Three-Dimensional Space: Three-Dimensional Space is how we refer to physical space that actually exists. This is the kind of space that is manipulated when a three-dimensional work of art is constructed. It is also the space we occupy. Two –Dimensional is space that exists on a flat surface. The illusion of depth, can be created in Two –Dimensional space, by manipulating space and other elements of art. The most common ways of doing this are to use overlapping, size, page position or linear perspective. Overlapping Linear Perspective Size and Page Position

Forms are objects that have height, width and depth. Form The figures shown here are two-dimensional drawings of forms. Forms can be drawn on a two-dimensional surface, but these drawings are not actually forms. **Three-dimensional forms** exist in real space and have actual height width and depth.

Organic and Geometric Forms Like line and shape, organic forms mimic natural lines and shapes while geometric forms contain straight lines and angles found in manmade structure.

Texture is the roughness or smoothness of a surface. Texture can be real, tactile texture (sandpaper), or visual texture (drawing of feathers).

Value is the appearance of light and dark in a work of art. Value ranges from black to white with an infinite number of grays in between. Colors also have value. For example, pink, is a lighter shade of red. Value is used to create the illusion of light and shadow in a composition. It is also another tool for creating the illusion of depth in a picture. The gray scale is a grid that shows a range of grays from white to black with a series of middle grays in between. white black middle gray dark middle gray light middle gray dark gray light gray

Contrast describes how many shades of gray are in a composition and how large the difference between light and dark in the composition is. The higher the contrast the fewer shades of gray there are and the stronger the difference between light and dark there is. The lower the contrast the grayer a composition looks. High Contrast Low Contrast By manipulating the contrast in a work of art well you can change the mood of a piece. Higher contrast tends to be more dramatic or edgy while lower contrast can be more dream like or surreal.

Shading and Creating Form Blending is a type of shading created by adjusting the pressure of the drawing tool, smudging and erasing. There are many methods for creating value in a drawing. Value can be used to shade an image giving it the appearance of volume, a light source and shadow. Shading can also give a picture the sense of depth and perspective.

Color is the light we see reflected from an object. It can affect the mood of a piece and add another dimension to an artwork. Color consists of three properties: Hue, the name of the color. Ex. Red or red- orange. Saturation, how bright or concentrated the color is. Value, how light or dark the color is. The colors in the color wheel get lighter as they get closer to the wheels center. The color wheel is the basis of color theory: The theory that explains which colors will result when different pigments are mixed.

The Primary Colors are red, yellow and blue. These colors can be mixed to make any other color. The Secondary Colors are Green, Orange and violet. These colors are made by mixing two primary colors. Tertiary Colors are colors created by mixing a secondary and a primary. Color basics Analogous Colors are colors that are next to each other on the color wheel. Cool Colors are colors that look cold and recede in space. These colors are mixed primarily from blue green and violet. Warm Colors are colors that look warm and come forward in space. These colors are mixed primarily from red, orange and yellow.

Color Basics Continued Opposite Colors or Complementary Colors are colors that are across from each other on the color wheel like red and green. Opposite colors mix to create Neutral Colors. Neutral colors are low in saturation. The more a color is mixed and the muddier it becomes the lower saturation it is. Mixing opposites to create neutrals. Saturated Neutral Saturated

Color Temperatures the degree in Kelvin which tells you the hue of a light source. These work together with white balance to allow the camera to mimic the colors the eye sees.

ELEMENTS OF ART CONTINUES:

The visual components of color, form, line, shape, space, texture, and value.
Line -- An element of art defined by a point moving in space. Line maybe two-or three-dimensional, descriptive, implied, or abstract
Shape An element of art that is two-dimensional, flat, or limited to height and width.
Form-- An element of art that is three-dimensional and encloses volume; includes height, width AND depth (as in a cube, a sphere, a pyramid, or a cylinder). Form may also be free flowing.
Value --The lightness or darkness of tones or colors. White is the lightest value; black is the darkest. The value halfway between these extremes is called middle gray.
Space --An element of art by which positive and negative areas are defined or a sense of depth achieved in a work of art.
Color-- An element of art made up of three properties: hue, value, and intensity.
- **Hue:** name of color

- **Value:** hue's lightness and darkness (a color's value changes when white or black is added)
- **Intensity:** quality of brightness and purity (high intensity= color is strong and bright; low intensity= color is faint and dull)

Texture An element of art that refers to the way things feel, or look as if they might feel if touched.

PRINCIPLES OF ART:

Balance, Emphasis, Movement, Proportion, Rhythm, Unity, and Variety; the means an artist uses to organize elements within a work of art.

Rhythm --A principle of design that indicates movement, created by the careful placement of repeated elements in a work of art to cause a visual tempo or beat.

Balance-- A way of combining elements to add a feeling of equilibrium or stability to a work of art. Major types are symmetrical and asymmetrical.

Symmetry: A form of balance achieved using identical balance compositional units on either side of a vertical axis within the picture plane.

Asymmetry: A form of balance attained when the visual units on balance either side of a vertical axis are not identical but are placed in positions within the picture plane so as to create a "felt" equilibrium of the total form concept.

Emphasis (contrast)
A way of combining elements to stress the differences between those elements.

Proportion -- A principle of design that refers to the relationship of certain elements to the whole and to each other.

Gradation ---A way of combining elements by using a series of gradual changes in those elements. (large shapes to small shapes, dark hue to light hue, etc.)

Harmony --A way of combining similar elements in an artwork to accent their similarities (achieved through use of repetitions and subtle gradual changes)

Variety ---A principle of design concerned with diversity or contrast. Variety is achieved by using different shapes, sizes, and/or colors in a work of art.

Movement --A principle of design used to create the look and feeling of action and to guide the viewer's eye throughout the work of art.

The 12 Principles of Animation

The Illusion of Life, Disney animators Ollie Johnston and Frank Thomas A BOOK WRITTEN IN 1981 introduced the twelve principles of animation. The two animators were part of Disney's "Nine Old Men," they were the core group who were instrumental in creating Disney's animation style. The twelve principles have now become widely recognized as a theoretical foundation for all artists working on animated video production.

In order, they consist of:
Squash and Stretch effect give animation an elastic life-like quality
Anticipation the preparation for the main action
Staging directs the most important elements in a scene draws the audience's attention this gives the story an effective advancement.
Straight Ahead Action and Pose-to-Pose: Straight ahead is drawn each frame of an action one after another as you go along. Pose to Pose starts in the beginning and end drawings of action, then the middle is filled in the frames.
Follow Through and Overlapping Action: The secondary elements (hair, clothing, fat) are

following-through on the primary element and overlapping its action.
Ease In, Ease Out: controlling the changing speeds of objects creates an animation that moves more smoothly and realistically
Arcs: are drawn curved trajectory that adds the illusion of life to an animated object in action.
Secondary Action: are gestures that support the main action to add more dimension to character animation.
Timing is about where on a timeline you put each frame of action.
Exaggeration: presents a character's features and actions in an extreme form for comedic or dramatic effect.
Solid Drawing: creating animated forms feel like they're in a three-dimensional space.
Appeal: real, interesting, and engaging characters

What is a rubric?

A systematic scoring guideline to evaluate students' performance (papers, speeches, problem solutions, portfolios, cases) using a detailed description of performance standards.

Used to get consistent scores across all students.

Allows students to be more aware of the expectations for performance and consequently improve their performance.

What questions do rubrics answer?

By what criteria should performance be judged?

Where should you look and what should you look for to judge successful performance?

What does the range in quality performance look like?

How do you determine validly, reliably, and fairly; what score should be given to a student and what that score means?

How should the different levels of quality be described and distinguished from one another?

What are some advantages of using rubrics?

Create objectivity and consistency

Clarify criteria in specific terms

Show how work will be evaluated and expectations

Promote student awareness provide benchmarks

Provide consistency when multiple instructors and/or TAs using it for scoring

What are the essential parts of a rubric?

A scale of points to be assigned in scoring a piece of work on a continuum of quality.

High numbers are typically assigned to the best work.

Descriptors for each level of performance that contain criteria and standards by which the performance will be judged

Indicators are often used in descriptors to provide examples or signs of performance in each level.

Criteria that describe the conditions that any performance must meet to be successful

Five categories to consider:

> **Impact** – the success of performance, given the purposes, goals and desired results
> **Work quality/Craftsmanship** – the overall polish, organization, and rigor of the work
> **Methods** – the quality of the procedures and manner of presentation, prior to and during performance
> **Content** – the correctness of the ideas, skills or materials used
> **Sophistication of the performance** – the relative complexity or maturity of the knowledge used

Should describe both strengths and errors (errors should be described particularly in lower levels of performance)

Standards that specify how well criteria must be met

Types of rubrics

Rubrics can be holistic or analytic, general or task specific

Holistic vs. analytic

Holistic rubrics provide a single score based on an overall impression of a student's performance on a task.

Advantages: quick scoring, provides overview of student achievement.

Disadvantages: does not provide detailed information, may be difficult to provide one overall score.

Analytic rubrics provide specific feedback along several dimensions.

Advantages: more detailed feedback, scoring more consistent across students and graders.

Disadvantage: time consuming to score.

General vs. task specific

General rubrics contain criteria that are general across tasks.

Advantage: can use the same rubric across different tasks.

Disadvantage: feedback may not be specific enough.

Task specific rubrics are unique to a specific task.

Advantage: more reliable assessment of performance on the task.

Disadvantage: difficult to construct rubrics for all specific tasks

Example: Tasks graphic presentation

    Scale 1 to 3

Criteria: Present graphics with details and exhibit colors that is appropriate as well as creative

    Scale 1: Graphics Poor use of graphics or no graphics

    Scale 2: Occasionally uses graphics, but rarely support presentation

    Scale 3: Graphics vary and relate to presentation

Graphics explain and reinforce message of presentation.

Color Theory

Color is the light we see reflected back from an object. It can affect the mood of a piece and add another dimension to an art work. Color consists of three properties:

Hue, the name of the color. Ex. Red or red-orange.

Saturation, how bright or concentrated the color is.

Value, how light or dark the color is. The colors in the color wheel get lighter as they get closer to the wheels center.

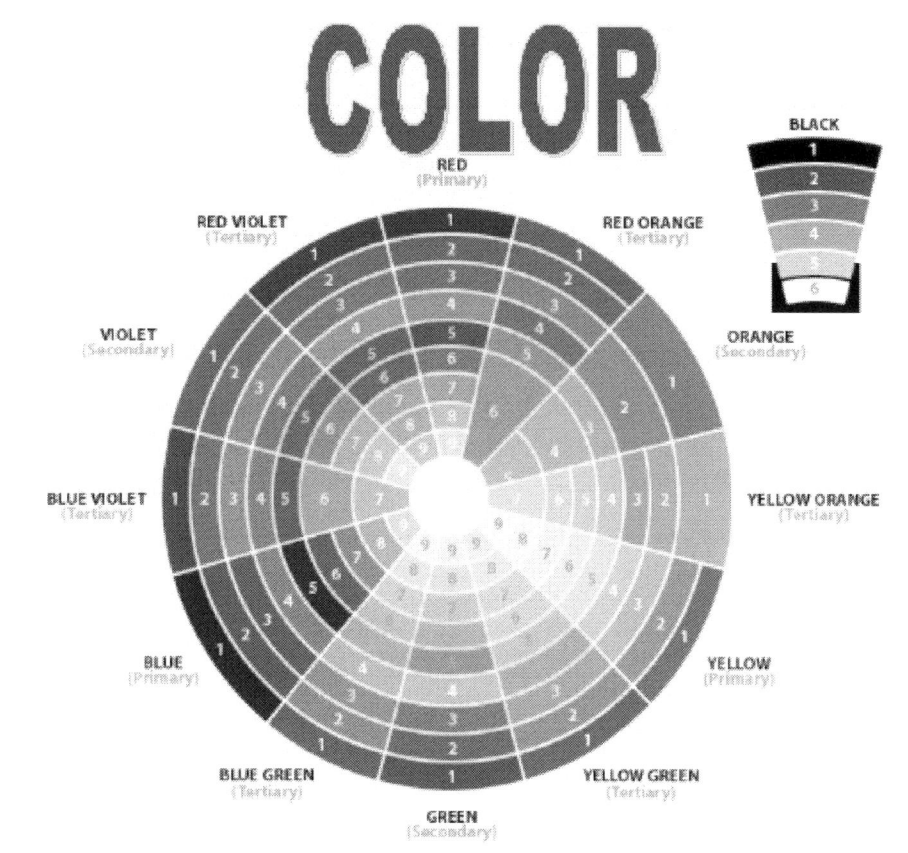

The color wheel is the basis of color theory: The theory that explains which colors will result when different pigments are mixed.

Color Basics Continued

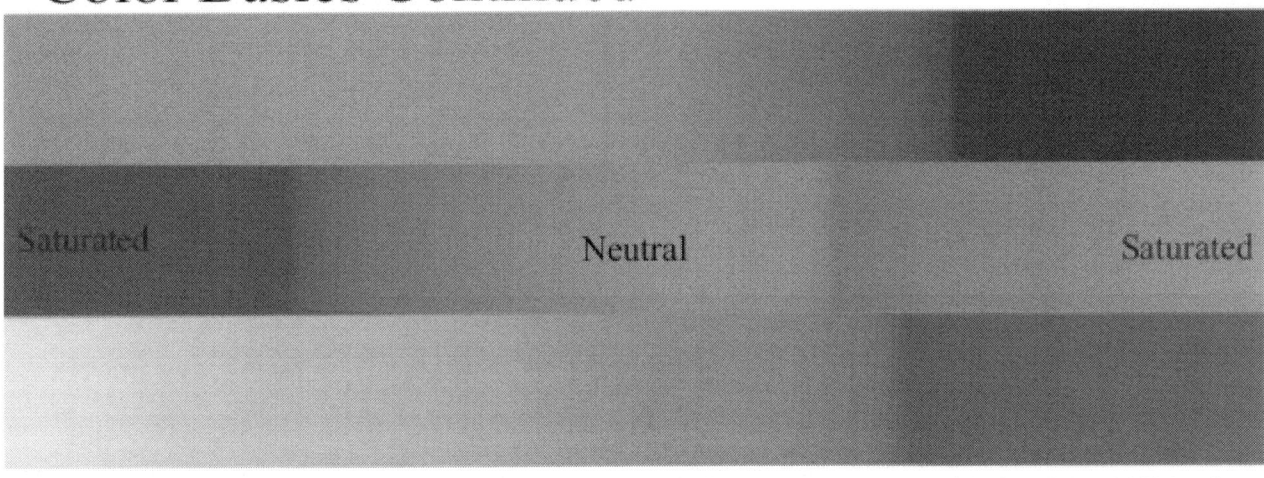

Saturated   Neutral   Saturated

Opposite Colors or Complementary Colors are colors that are across from each other on the color wheel like red and green. Opposite colors mix to create Neutral Colors. Neutral colors are low in saturation. The more a color is mixed and the muddier it becomes the lower saturation it is.

Mixing opposites to create neutrals.

Shading and Creating Form

There are many methods for creating value in a drawing. Value can be used to shade an image giving it the appearance of volume, a light source and shadow. Shading can also give a picture the sense of depth and perspective.

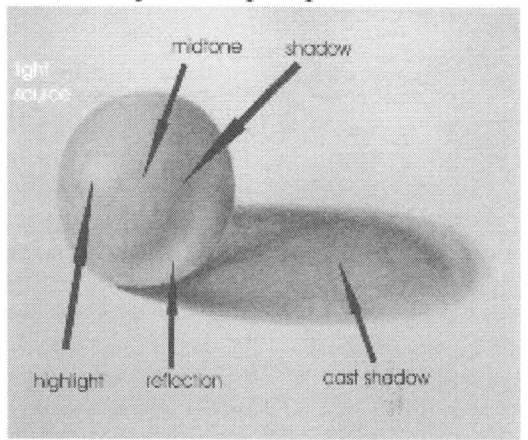

hatching - a row of lines, all facing in the same direction. More dense and concentrated in the areas that appear darker.

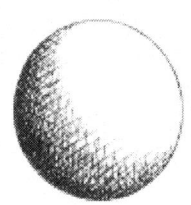

cross-hatching - similar to hatching, except with the addition of criss-crossing lines.

contour-hatching - follows the contour, or curve or outline, of the object. In this case, the hatching is rounded to match the shape of the circle.

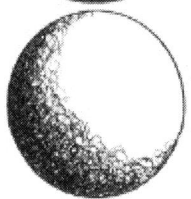

scumbling - tiny, squiggly circular lines - sort of like "controlled scribbling"

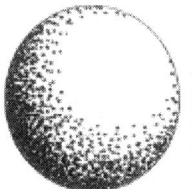

stippling - placing many, many dots on the paper to indicate shading. Probably the most time consuming of all the methods, but creates some neat effects.

Blending is a type of shading created by adjusting the pressure of the drawing tool, smudging and erasing.

37

MONOCHROMATIC COLORS

Monochromatic color scheme means "One Color". It is a color scheme that uses only one hue and all the values (tints and shades) of that hue.

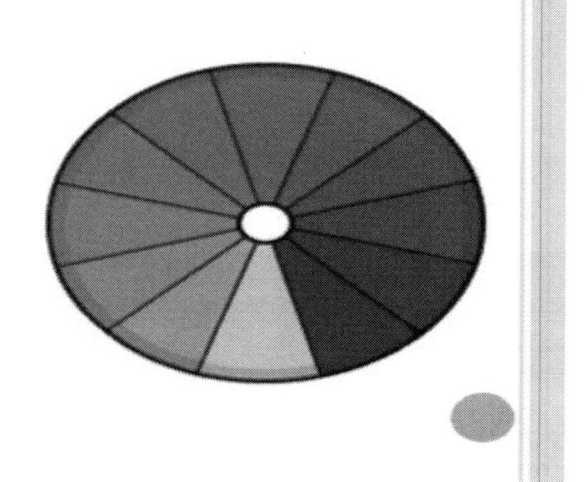

Color Theory

Colors

Shading

Monochromatic

Triad - based on three hue equidistant apart on the color wheel

May include any tint, shade, or pastel of the hues being used and the addition of any achromatic

Tetrad – based on four hues equidistant apart on the color wheel

May include any tint, shade, or pastel of the hues being used and the addition of any achromatic.

Box 3D Modeling

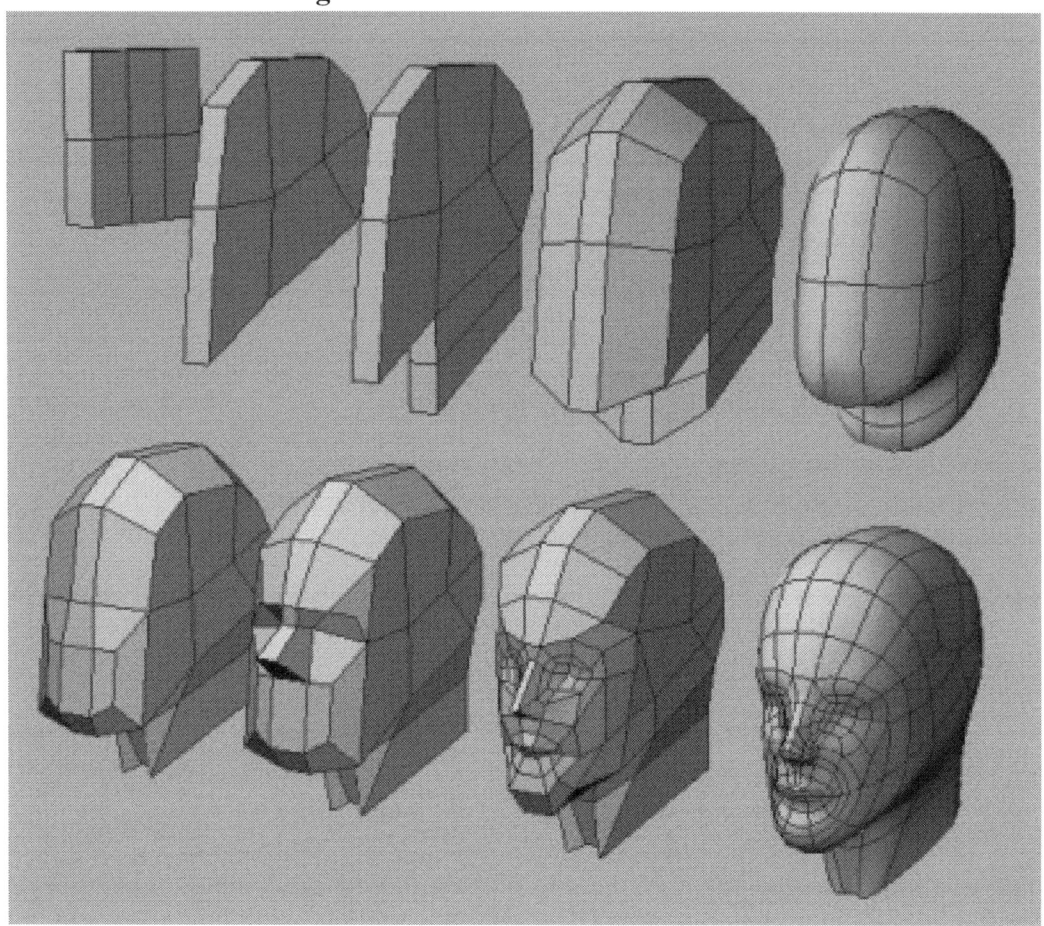

Box modeling is a 3D modeling technique in which the artist begins with a low-resolution primitive (typically a cube or sphere) and modifies the shape by extruding, scaling, or rotating faces and edges. Detail is added to a 3D primitive either by manually adding edge loops, or by subdividing the entire surface uniformly to increase polygonal resolution by an order of magnitude.

CMYK (cyan, magenta, yellow, black)

Use: Printing

Use in offset and digital printing. Ideal for full-color brochures, flyers, posters and post cards, etc.

RGB (red, green, blue)

Use: Onscreen

The most commonly used color profile in the world of computers, TV screens and mobile devices is RGB.

RGB is the process by which colors are rendered onscreen by using combinations of red, green and blue.

HEX (hexadecimal color)

Use: Onscreen for websites

Designers and developers use HEX colors in web design. A HEX color is expressed as a six-digit combination of numbers and letters defined by its mix of red, green and blue (RGB).

PMS (Pantone® Matching System)

Use: Printing

For offset printing only. Ideal for stationery. Often used in one or two-color jobs. Also used as spot colors on premium brochures in addition to four-color process.

A spot color is a special premixed ink that is used instead of, or in addition to, process inks, and that requires its own printing plate on a printing press.

Grayscale

Grayscale uses tints of black to represent an object. Every grayscale object has a brightness value ranging from 0% (white) to 100% (black). Images produced using black-and-white or grayscale scanners are typically displayed in grayscale.

Competency 005: The Technology Applications teacher demonstrates knowledge of principles of typography, modeling and page layout using appropriate graphic tools to create a variety of products.

Basic Productivity Tools

Basic productivity tools are computer software programs which allow a user to create specific items quickly and easily as opposed to creating the same items by hand. We learned about three specific productivity tools:

Word Processing. Word Processing is a software program that creates documents using text and/or graphics. An example would be Microsoft Word.

Spreadsheets. Spreadsheets quickly organize numerical information and allows the creator to input formulas into the spreadsheet for easy calculation. An example would be Microsoft Excel.

Databases. Databases allow the user to save collections of information in one easily accessible place. This allows the user to find information about a specific topic much faster versus searching the internet. An example of a database would be SQL or Oracle.

Microsoft Office is a common productivity software package which includes Microsoft Word, Excel, and PowerPoint. Pages is the Mac productivity tool equivalent to Microsoft word. Productivity tools are used all over the world by lots of different people for many reasons. Accountants use Excel to create ledgers, teachers use Word to create tests, and Marketers use PowerPoint for presentations and slide shows.

The differences between Productivity Software and Instructional Software is that productivity Software helps users create products such as a word document, excel spreadsheet, power point, etc.; while Instructional Software has already been produced, cannot be changed, and is used to reinforce a lesson.

Typography

Typography is the art and/or technique behind arranging type, where type means the letters and characters that you see in printed material. A font is the style of letter or character it would be something like Times New Roman.

Stroke

The stroke is simply one of the lines that comprise any given letter.

Stem

The stem is a type of stroke, the basic unit of the parts of a character. The stem is usually the main and vertical stroke in a letter.

Serif

A serif is the little extra stroke or curves, at the ends of letters. Serif is used in print

Sans-serif

"Sans" literally means "without", and a sans serif font does not include any extra stroke at the ends of the letters. Sans-Serif is used on the Web.

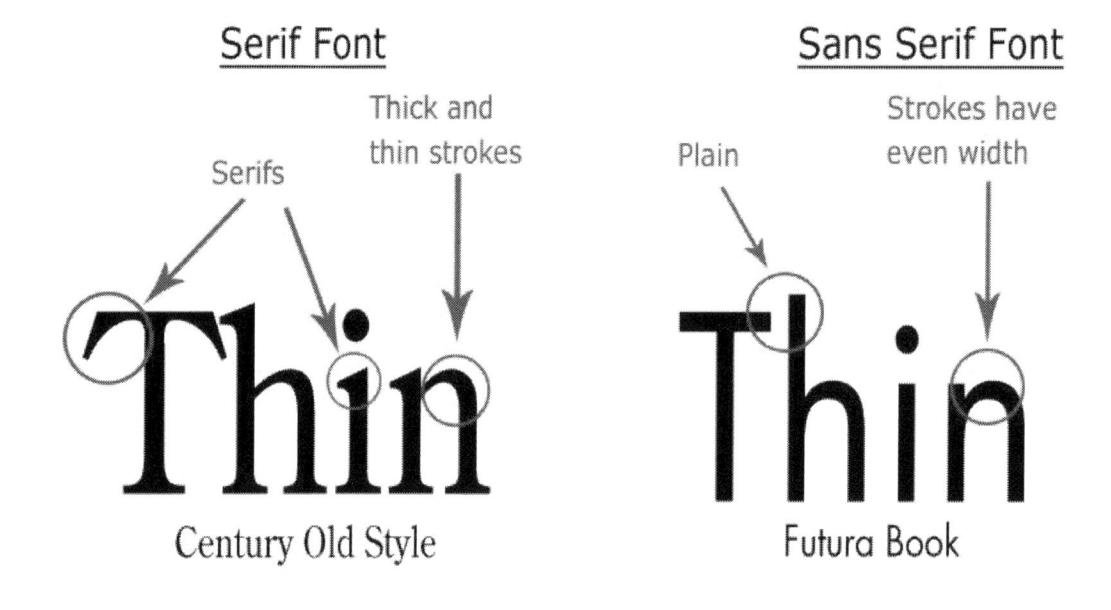

Hierarchy

Typographic hierarchy is an essential part of any design or layout it is on any website, newspaper or magazine.

Kerning

Kerning refers to the space between two specific letters (or other characters: numbers, punctuation, etc.) and the process of adjusting that space improves legibility.

Tracking is similar to kerning in that it refers to the spacing between letters or characters. However, instead of focusing on the spacing between individual letters (kerning), tracking measures space between groups of letters.

Tracking:
VAST.   V A S T .

Kerning:
VAST. VAST.

Leading determines the amount of space between vertical lines in a paragraph.

Drop Cap

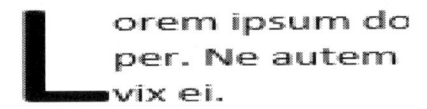

L orem ipsum do
per. Ne autem
vix ei.

Ne partem omi
consequat elab
homero compr

A drop cap (dropped capital) is a large capital letter used as a decorative element at the beginning of a paragraph or section.

Principles of Design

The principles of design are balance, proximity, alignment, repetition, contrast and white space. The principles govern the relationships between the elements used in the design and organize the composition as a whole.

Successful design incorporates the use of the principles to communicate the intended message effectively.

Balance is an equal distribution of weight. In terms of graphics, this applies to visual weight. Each element on a layout has visual weight that is determined by its size, darkness or lightness, and thickness of lines.

The Principle of Proximity states that you group related items together, move them physically close to each other so the related items are one cohesive group rather than a bunch of unrelated bits. The basic purpose of proximity is to organize.

The Principle of Alignment states, "Nothing should be placed on the page arbitrarily. Every item should have a visual connection with something else on the page. "When items are aligned, the result is a stronger cohesive unit. The basic purpose of alignment is to unify and organize

The Principle of Repetition states, "Repeat some aspect of the design throughout the entire piece." The repetitive element may be a bold font, a thick line, a certain bullet, color, design element, particular format, spatial relationship, etc. Repetition helps organize the information; it guides the reader and helps to unify parts of the design.

Contrast is the most effective way to add visual interest to your page. Contrast is also crucial to the organization of information - a reader should always be able to glance at a document and instantly understand what's going on.

Principle of White Space:

"White space is the art of nothing. White space is the absence of text and graphics." There are two types of white space, the undefined white space, which is what you get when you open a new document, and active white space, which occurs when an object is placed in an undefined white space.

Competency 006: The Technology Applications teacher knows how to use graphics, animation and page design to produce products that convey a specified message to an intended audience.

What is 3D?

A Cartesian coordinate system is basically a fancy way of describing the X and Y axes remember high school geometry graph paper. The graph paper the X axis being horizontal, and the Y-axis being vertical, right. It is very much similar in the world of 3D, with one exception – there's a third axis: Z, which represents depth.

3D Modeling

The process of creating a 3D representation of any surface or object by manipulating polygons, edges, and vertices in simulated 3D space. You've seen the results of 3D modeling in movies, animations, and video games that are filled with fantastical and imaginative creatures and structures.

3D modeling can be produced utilizing a specialized 3D production software that allow an artist to create and deform polygonal surfaces or by scanning real-world objects into a set of data points that can be used to represent the object digitally. Simple terms any object that can be represented on a three-axis system is 3D.

Animation Terminology:

ANIMATIC A more advanced storyboard using proxy models to rough out basic animation and camera shots. (Film industry term)

ANTI-ALIASING Over-sampling methods for avoiding the unwanted visual effects or artefacts caused by limited display resolution. These aliasing effects include 'jaggies' (stair-casing along diagonal lines), moiré effects, and temporal aliasing (strobing) in animated scenes.

ANIMATION The process of developing the actions (poses, timing, motion) of objects. Animation methods include key-frame animation, path animation, non-linear character animation, and motion capture animation. Animations are sequences of frames.

ARMATURE Available in 3D (and some 2D, such as Flash) animation software, this is an arrangement of links called "bones" (which can be rigid or flexible) that make up the equivalent of a skeleton.

AXIS One of three vectors (X, Y, and Z) that define the three dimensions of a scene. Often defined as local space, object space, origin axis or world space.

CAD Computer Aided Design. Designing 2D and 3D work using a computer as a tool.

CAMERA Like a real-world camera, the 3D camera frames the view of a scene by tracking, tumbling, panning, and zooming. Unlike a real-world camera, the 3D camera does not automatically capture lighting, motion blur, and other effects - these effects must be explicitly created and tuned for realistic output.

CG Computer generated. Design output via a computer.

CGI Computer generated Imagery. Design output via a computer.

CODEC Abbreviation of "compressor/de-compressor". This is the term used to reference the way that software programs handle different movie files, such as Quick Time, AVI, etc. The CODEC can control image quality and can assign the amount of space given to the movie file.

COLOR DEPTH The number of bits used to represent a color. For example, an 8-bit image uses $2^8=256$ colors. The bits build up the three primary colors red, green and blue. The following table indicates the number of colors an image can have.

    8-bit = 2^8 = 256

    16-bit = 2^{16} = 65536

    24-bit = 2^{24} = 16 million

    32-bit = 2^{32} = 4.3 billion

COMPOSITING ('COMPING') The process of combining two or more images to form a new image. In video, compositing is the process of combining two or more video sequences to form a new video sequence.

DEPTH OF FIELD (DOF) A photographic term for the range of distances within which objects will be sharply focused. **(Objects outside of this range appear blurred or out of focus)**

DIFFUSE Surfaces reflect (or scatter) light, and color in many angles. This type of surface causes light and color to spread freely.

DYNAMICS A branch of physics that describes how objects move using physical rules to simulate the natural forces that act upon them. Dynamic simulations are difficult to achieve with traditional key-frame animation techniques, but new technology lets you set up the conditions and constraints that you want to occur, and then automatically solves how to animate the objects in the scene.

ENCODING The process of converting uncompressed image/s to a new format, usually compressed. (e.g. Mpeg, MP4, QuickTime, WMV, H264 etc.)

FPS Frames per second. The number of single frames needed to be displayed in a second to achieve smooth animation (usually 25 fps).

FRACTAL A three-dimensional random function with a particular frequency distribution. Fractal textures are useful for simulating many natural phenomena, such as rock surfaces, clouds, or flames.

FRAME In animation, a still image and the basic unit of time measurement. Typically, 25 frames of animation are required for one second of PAL video.

KEYFRAME A frame in an animation where at least one property of at least one object in the scene is precisely defined.

LAYER As the name suggests, a layer is a group of graphic items that can not only be shown or hidden but can appear above or below other layers.

MOTION CAPTURE In animation, the recording of joint positions and rotations from movements performed typically by a human actor. This information is then applied to a CG skeleton to simulate real-life motion on a character.

NTSC National Television Standards Committee. The standard for composite video in North America, Japan, and most of South America. 30fps, 720x486 with a pixel aspect of 0.9

OPENGL A widely used 3D graphics language.

PAL Phase Alternate Line. The industry standard for composite video in most of Europe. 25fps, 720x576 with pixel aspect ratio of 1.0667.

PARTICLES In dynamics, a point displayed as a dot, streak, sphere, or other effect. You can animate the display and movement of particles with various techniques. Typically used in large quantities to create effects like rain and explosions.

PIXEL A picture element. The smallest controllable segment of computer or video display or image.

POLYGON Cross-platform industry standard for constructing geometry. N-sided facet defined by 3 or more vertices in space. A polygonal object can be closed, open, or made up of shells, which are disjointed pieces of geometry. Often referred to as a mesh.

RENDERING the process of turning a 3D digital model, with its associated textures, lighting, and a virtual camera, into a 2D image. Images can be photo realistic, cartoon style, hand sketch style, or any combination of these depending on the computational processes used to combine the lighting with the geometry and the image textures.

RIGGING The process of creating the controls for an armature that in turn controls a mesh. This not only includes creating the bones that make up the armature, but also defining each bone's influence on surrounding vertices, limits to the bones' rotation and movement, the way that one bones controls the next, and the amount of flexibility in the bone itself. A finished rig is entirely composed of graphic elements; the original bones and armature will be hidden.

ROTOSCOPE The tracing of film from live action footage, sometimes the whole of the live action image and sometimes only points to match registration in the animation.

SCENE A scene is a file containing all the information necessary to identify and position all of the models, lights and cameras for rendering. A scene can be identified with the 3D coordinate space in which rendering takes place. This space is often called the "global" coordinate space, as opposed to the "local" coordinate spaces associated with each individual object in the scene.

SEQUENCE – A series of Scenes, usually occurring at one time and location dealing with the development of a single, main plot point.

SKELETON In animation, a structure that consists of joints and their bones, used to create hierarchical, articulated deformation effects on deformable objects.

SPLIT SCREEN – Multiple images that appear on screen at the same time.

STAGING – The positioning of all elements in a scene so the action will be clearly represented. Usually done by Layout but also paid attention to and often refined by Animators.

STORYBOARD A series of drawings used in the early planning an animation.

TIMELINE A horizontal window, generally placed at the bottom of the screen in a horizontal format, that shows scene animation on a time axis.

TWEENING Short for "in-betweening", this is the process of creating intermediate drawings between keyframes.

2D Animation

Types of 2D Animation

Cel Animation - (traditional animation) is based on a series of frames or cels in which the object is redrawn in each consecutive cel to depict motion. Cel comes from the word celluloid (a transparent sheet material) which was first used to draw the images and place them on a stationary background.

Path Animation - Path Based animation is the simplest form of animation and the easiest to learn. It moves an object along a predetermined path on the screen. The path could be a straight line, or it could include any number of curves. Often the object does not change, although it might be resized or reshaped.

Onion Skinning - Onion Skinning is used in the process of creating cel animations. It allows you to see a faint outline of the previous cel so you can draw the changes for the next cel.

Tweening is also used in 2D animation from the word - "in between" tweening is a method where the first cel of an animation and the last cel of animation are selected and the animation program calculates all the cells in between.

Scripting Language are programming language such as, python, C++ etc but this programming language have been utilized to build software that has a good user interface (UI) in which animation, games can be developed with ease.

There are various types of Graphic Designs that are used for specific projects.

Logo: A logo is a graphic mark, or a symbol used to identify the company, product or brand.

Publication Graphic Design are: Newspapers Books Newsletters Directories Annual Reports Magazines Catalogs

Website Graphic Design: Design websites

Advertising Graphic Design Advertising design refers to creating and organizing the visual artwork used in the advertisements for product and services.

Brochure Design: Brochures are a great marketing tool for any company to provide the information about its products and services.

Stationery Design: design of the stationary such as, letterheads, business cards, folders, envelopes, etc.,

Lighting Techniques

KEY light is also known as the main light of a scene or subject. This means it's normally the strongest light in each scene or photo.

FILL IN light "fill in" and remove the dark, shadowy areas that your key light creates. It is noticeably less intense and placed in the opposite direction of the key light, this is for adding more dimension to the scene.

Because the aim of fill lighting is to eliminate shadows, it's advisable to place it a little further and/or diffuse it with a reflector (placed around 3/4 opposite to the key light) to create softer light that spreads out evenly. Many scenes do well with just the key and fill studio lighting as they are enough to add noticeable depth and dimension to any object.

BACKLIGHTING is used to create a three-dimensional scene, which is why it is also the last to be added in a three-point lighting setup. This also faces your subject—a little higher from behind to separate your subject from the background.

As with fill lighting, backlight should be diffuse, so it becomes less intense and covers a wider area of your subject.

SOFT lighting doesn't refer to any lighting direction, but it's a technique, nonetheless. Cinematographers make use of soft lighting (even when creating directional lighting with the techniques above) for both aesthetic and situational reasons: to reduce or eliminate harsh shadows, create drama, replicate subtle lighting coming from outside, or all the above.

HARD light can be sunlight or a strong light source. It's usually unwanted, but it certainly has cinematic benefits. Hard lighting can be created with direct sunlight or a small, powerful light source. Despite it creating harsh shadows, hard lighting is great for drawing attention to the main subject or to an area of the scene, highlighting the subject's contour, and creating a strong silhouette.

AMBIENT light Using artificial light sources is still the best way to create a well-lit scene that's closely similar to or even better than what we see in real life. However, there's no reason not to make use of ambient or available lights that already exist in the shooting location,

HIGH KEY light refers to a style of lighting used to create a very bright scene that's visually shadowless, often close to overexposure. Lighting ratios are ignored so all light sources would have pretty much the same intensity. This technique is used in many movies, TV sitcoms, commercials, and music videos today, but it first became popular during the classic Hollywood period in the 1930s and 40s.

MOTIVATED lighting is used to imitate a natural light source, such as sunlight, moonlight, and street lamps at night. It's also the kind of lighting that enhances practical lights, should the director or cinematographer wish to customize the intensity or coverage of the latter using a separate light source.

LOW KEY lighting for a scene would mean a lot of shadows and possibly just one strong key light source. The focus is on the use of shadows and how it creates mystery, suspense, or drama for a scene and character instead of on the use of lighting, which makes it great for horror and thriller films.

3D Lighting

Sphere light, also known as Point light. It creates a rays-of-light source in every direction from a single small point in the 3D environment.

Spot light describes exactly what it does – it puts the object in the spotlight by lighting directly onto it from a cone-shaped source of light and creating a circle around the scene with shadows inside. It casts a focused ray of light onto the 3D scene, to make it stand out from other elements in the environment. It resembles a street lamp or an indoor lamp.

Tube light similarly to the Sphere light, the Tube generates rays of light to every direction. With the edges being rounded, the light creates wide shadows, with transition from hard to soft.

Directional light casts rays of light directly onto the object that is placed in the 3D scene. It makes visible the hard shadows caused by the directional impact of the light on the object.

Rectangle light the center part of the light has increased intensity, which fades out towards the edges of the light. This light creates soft shadows behind the object, which are caused by spreading the rays of light to the sides.

Hemisphere light offers a combination of two different colors smoothly transitioning from one to the other and creating a gradient feeling of the whole project.

Domain III — Digital Communications and Multimedia

Competency 007: The Technology Applications teacher knows how to produce and distribute digital video and multimedia products.

Film & TV Production Roles and Departments

KEY CREATIVE TEAM

Producer

The producer initiates, coordinates, supervises, and controls matters such as raising funding, hiring key personnel, contracting and arranging for distributors. The producer is involved throughout all phases of the process from development to completion of a project.

Director

The director is responsible for overseeing the creative aspects of a film, including controlling the content and flow of the film's plot, directing the performances of actors, selecting the locations in which the film will be shot, and managing technical details such as the positioning of cameras, the use of lighting, and the timing and content of the film's soundtrack.

Screenwriter

Screenwriters or scriptwriters are responsible for researching the story, developing the narrative, writing the screenplay, and delivering it, in the required format, to the Producers.

PRODUCTION DEPARTMENT

Executive Producer

An executive producer is usually an investor in the project or someone who has facilitated the funding of the project. There may be multiple executive producers on a project, depending on the financing arrangements.

CAMERA DEPARTMENT

Director of Photography/Cinematographer

The director of photography is the head of the camera and lighting department of the film. The DoP makes decisions on lighting and framing of scenes in conjunction with the film's director.

Camera Operator

The camera operator operates the camera under the direction of the director of photography, or the film director, to capture the scenes on film. Depending on the camera format being used for filming (e.g. film or digital), a director of photography may not operate the camera, but sometimes these two roles are combined.

SOUND DEPARTMENT

Production Sound Mixer (Sound Recordist)

The production sound mixer is head of the sound department on set, responsible for recording all sound during filming. This involves the choice of microphones, operation of a sound recording device, and sometimes the mixing of audio signals in real time.

Boom Operator (Boom Swinger)

The boom operator is responsible for microphone placement and movement during filming. The boom operator uses a boom pole to position the microphone above or below the actors, just out of the camera's frame.

ELECTRICAL DEPARTMENT

Gaffer

The gaffer is the head of the electrical department, responsible for the design and execution of the lighting plan for a production. Sometimes the gaffer is credited as "Chief Lighting Technician".

POST PRODUCTION

Film Editor (Offline Editor for video productions) Assembles the various shots into a coherent film, working closely with the director.

Assistant Editor

Assists the editor by collecting and organizing all the elements needed for the edit.

OTHER PRODUCTION CREW

Composer

The composer is responsible for writing the musical score for a film.

Storyboard Artist

Visualizes stories using sketches on paper. Quick pencil drawings and marker renderings are two of the most common traditional techniques, although nowadays Flash, Photoshop and specialist storyboard software applications are being used more often.

Pre-Production, Production and Post-Production

Pre-production -video or film production such as the script, casting, location scouting, equipment and crew, and the shot list all happen during pre-production.

Production

Production is the actual filming of the video.

Post-Production the work that is done after the filming is complete this includes organizing, cutting, coloring and editing the footage captured in production.

Timeline for production of film/video including animation, documentary.

Pre-Production

1. Set a budget
2. Develop creative idea
3. Write the script
4. Create storyboard
5. Find the Location and equipment to be used
6. Obtain Permits
7. Find the Cast
8. Schedule the Shoot

Understanding Depth of Field

- **In this graphic, the black line at 15' is critically sharp. This is where the lens is focused.
The yellow area would appear 'acceptably sharp'...
The yellow area represents the Depth Of**

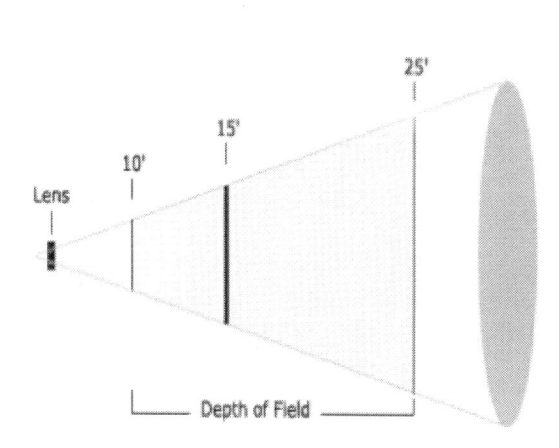

Camera Perspective with content selection and framing.

Understanding Depth of Field sometimes referred to DOF. The depth of field (DOF) is the front-to-back area of a photograph in which the image is razor sharp clear. DOF there is a point of optimum focus in a zone on a photograph where the object is very clear. Focus enables you to isolate a subject and specifically draw the viewer's eye to exactly where you want it. Depth of Focus is determined by three factors – aperture sizes/f-stop being used, distance from the lens, and the focal length of the lens.

DISTANCE • Closer to subject is to the camera lens, the less depth of field • increase the distance from subject, increase in the depth of field • With close-up or macro photography, a very shallow depth of field

F/STOP • A large f-stop or bigger aperture opening, a smaller depth of field • A smaller f-stop will give a larger depth of field • For less depth of field you open up and for more depth of field you stop down

FOCAL LENGTH • Shorter focal length lenses yield a greater DOF than longer focal lengths • a wide-angle lens will increase the DOF and when using a telephoto will decrease the DOF.

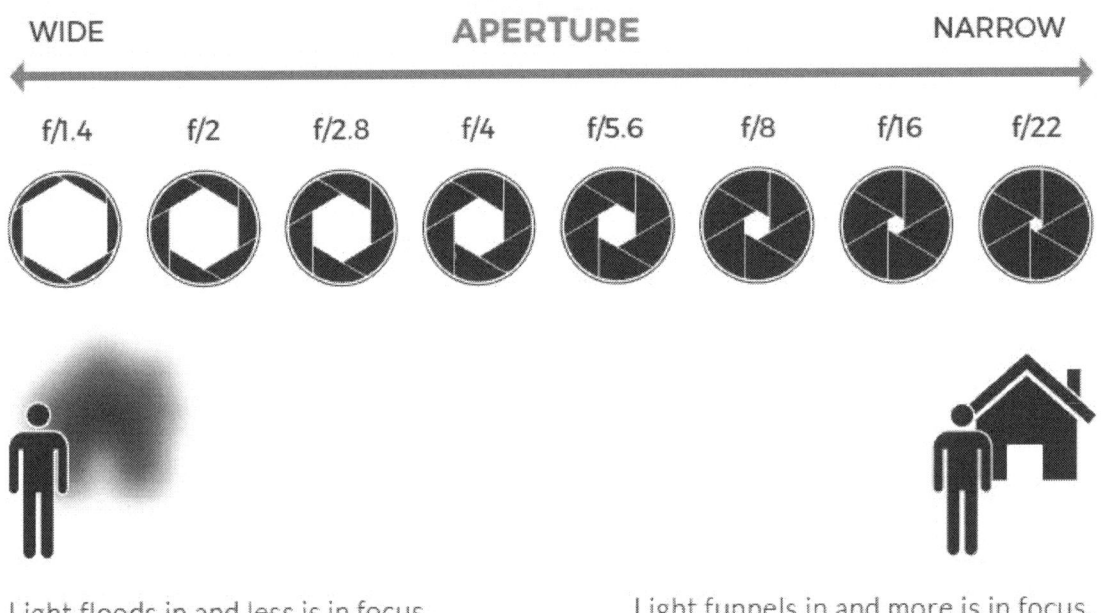

WIDE ← APERTURE → NARROW

f/1.4   f/2   f/2.8   f/4   f/5.6   f/8   f/16   f/22

Light floods in and less is in focus. Shallow depth of field occurs.

Light funnels in and more is in focus. Deeper depth of field occurs.

Aperture VS Shutter Speed (SS) • The aperture and shutter- speed combinations shown • Allow the same amount of light to enter the camera but result in different images • Smaller apertures extend the zone of sharp focus, and slow shutter speeds show blurred movement

The Camera Angles and Movement

Bird's-Eye View, the camera is placed above the subject, looking down toward the subject and the ground. This kind of shot can seem disorienting because it is rarely the way audiences themselves see the world. Because of this, directors often use the bird's-eye view when they want to make dramatic comment on a character or scene. Photographing from this point of view can make viewers feel as though they are superior to the subject

Worm's Eye or Low Angle, looking upwards, has the opposite effect of a high angle shot. It tends to focus attention on the size and significance of a character or object. Often directors will use this kind of shot to symbolically announce the power and authority of one of their characters without literally telling the audience this information.

High Angle, looking downwards, tends to draw attention to the importance of the environment or setting for a scene. High angle shots also tend to make characters look small and are often used by directors to symbolically suggest in-significance or withering authority.

Oblique Angle is shot by literally tilting the camera frame. It can be used to suggest a sense of "crookedness" and anxiety, or, in the case of some television news shows and music video programs, a sense of playfulness.

Movement of the Camera

Pan turns the camera to the left or right, focusing attention on an object or subject being followed.

Tilt pivots the camera upwards or downwards, often to survey surroundings, and frequently mimics the sight of the character in point of view shots.

Zoom doesn't really move the camera at all, it simply enlarges or reduces the proportion of the frame taken up by a person or object. In doing so, the zoom can focus attention on a detail, but over-use of the zoom is often distracting.

Dolly is the movement of the camera towards or from an object or subject. Dollies are often used in point of view shots to give the audience the impression of approaching someone or something with the character.

Competency 008: The Technology Applications teacher demonstrates knowledge of current practice, future trends and procedural protocols in the use of audio/video and digital publications.

Producing audio and video: Planning

'Before you hit record, planning is everything'

Effective planning is the most critical part in the production of educational media. Most people skip right to the shooting step before doing any planning. To get a good quality recording, an individual need to carefully plan their finished product and the steps towards producing it.

Make sure to consider the following:

1. Understand the purpose

2. Brainstorm

3. Prepare

The most appropriate file type based on universally recognized file formats for audio, video and digital publications:

MP3- is a lossy format. That means that an MP3 file does not contain 100% of the original audio information. Instead, MP3 files use perceptual coding. In other words, that means it removes the information that your ear doesn't notice thereby making the file smaller. The reason lossy formats are used over RAW is that RAW audio files are too large to travel over the internet at any great speed. By using lossy formats, it enables even dial up users to download mp3 files at a reasonable speed. RAW file formats generally require 176,000 bytes per second compared to a lossy format which requires 17,600. The difference is massive and so are the download times

MP4- files are superior to MP3 in terms of the scale of compression and audio quality. The M4A file uses Apple's codec and resides within the MPEG-4 container. The main benefit of M4A is that files are compressed but are lossless. This means they can be decoded back to the original quality they were at the point of compression. Another benefit of M4A files are that do not carry any Digital Rights Management (DRM) protection associated with other files meaning they are less restricted. MP4 is comprised mainly of audio but can also include video.

WAV-files are the standard digital audio format in Windows. Using the .WAV file extension, 8- or 16-bit samples can be taken at rates of 11,025 Hz, 22,050 Hz and 44,100 Hz. The highest quality being the 16-bit at 44,100 HZ, this highest level is the sampling rate of an audio CD and uses 88KB of storage per second.

MOV- files use a **(Apple)** proprietary compression algorithm and each track that is held within the file is made up of an encoded media stream or a reference to a media stream that is in another file - this allows the embedding of existing media. **QuickTime** player which was developed and created by Apple allows a user to open and play .MOV files and later version of QuickTime Player, such as QuickTime Pro allows the user to edit and export .MOV files.

OGG- format is actually a container that potentially allows for different streams of audio, video and metadata. It is open source file. Ogg Vorbis is the compression format. It provides medium to high quality audio at between 16 and 128 kbps/channel and is better quality sound than mp3. The OGG file type is a lossy codec which means that data is discarded as part of the compression technique, resulting in a smaller file size.

AVI -stands for Audio Video Interleave. Files of this format have an .avi extension. Developed by Microsoft in 1992, it has become so widespread that many people consider it the de-facto standard for storing video and audio information on PC. AVI combines audio and video into a single file in a standard container to allow simultaneous playback. **AVI is a derivative of the Resource Interchange File Format (RIFF)**, which divides a file's data into blocks, or chunks. Each chunk is identified by a Four CC tag.

Common audio and video techniques

Basic Principles of Sound

When we speak, vibrations, called sound waves, are created. Sound waves have a recurring pattern, or an analog wave pattern called a waveform. This analog wave pattern represents the volume and frequency of a sound.

Amplitude: Distance between the valley and the peak of a waveform; determines volume.

Volume is measured in decibels (dB)Decibel (dB) is a logarithmic unit used to describe a ratio. One dB is close to Just Noticeable Difference (JND) for sound level. Frequency: Number of peaks that occur in one second measured by the distance between the peaks; determines pitch.

Analog sound is a continuous stream of sound waves. For sound to be included in multimedia applications, analog sound must be converted to digital form.

Digitizing (or sound sampling): the process of converting analog sound to numbers.

Digital Audio: An analog sound that has been converted to numbers.

Sound sampling converts analog sound to digital audio. During digitizing, sound samples are taken at regular time instants. Time instants are discrete. Sound samples (the volumes of sound at time instants) cannot be stored precisely. Instead, only quantified values can be stored. The feasible quantified values are known as quantization levels.

The number of quantization levels is related to the quality of digital audio. If more quantization levels are allowed, the difference between the original value and the quantified value will be smaller and we will get a better quality of the digital representation. However, this would also mean a higher cost for storage and processing of these values inside a computer (disks of larger capacity and more powerful CPUs are required)

Sound Quality

Factors that determine the sound quality of digital audio sample rate audio resolution. Sample rate. Number of sound samples taken per second. Also known as sampling rate Measured in kilohertz (kHz), Common values: 11 kHz, 22 kHz, 44 kHz CD quality: 44 kHz

Sound Quality Audio resolution

Also known as sample size or bit resolution. Number of binary bits used to represent each sound sample. As the audio resolution increases, the quality of the digital audio also improves. Audio resolution determines the accuracy with which sound can be digitized. Common values: 8 bits, 16 bits, CD quality: 16 bits.

Audio Compression: Similar to image compression (refer to Unit 5), mathematical algorithms are used to reduce file sizes. File size is the primary consideration when using audio files on the Web. Compression is beneficial for storing and transferring audio files.

Audio Compression Different: compression schemes are available for different file formats, and some file formats include the compression scheme within the format itself. The compression scheme applied impacts both the quality of audio file and the file size.

Digital Audio File Size
Ex: When a 6 MB audio file is compressed to 3 MB, the compression ratio is (6 / 3) = 2

Downloaded vs. Streamed
Web audio: downloaded or streamed. Downloaded audio file must be entirely saved to the user's computer before it can be played. .Streaming: a more advanced process that allows audio file to be played as it is downloading (i.e. before the entire file is transferred to the user's computer)If we want our audio files to be streamed over the Internet, the web-hosting service must support streaming.

If the user's computer receives streaming audio data more quickly than required, the excess data will be stored in a buffer. If the user's computer receives streaming audio data slower than required, the data stored in the buffer will be used. If the buffer becomes empty, the user will experience a break.

Two types of streamed audio:

On demand. Streamed audio is stored on a server for a long period of time and is available for transmission at a user's request.

Live: Live streams are only available at one particular time. **Example: live radio program.**

Audio Editing Basic Techniques

Basic sound editing operations. Multiple tracks editing. Edit and combine multiple tracks and then merge the tracks and export them in a "final mix" to a single audio file. Trimming Remove "dead air" or blank space from the front of a recording and any unnecessary extra time off the end. Splicing and assembly. Remove the extraneous noises that inevitably creep into a recording. Volume adjustments. Provide a consistent volume level.

Format conversion. Import and save files in various formats. Resampling or down sampling. Increase or reduce sample rates. Fade-ins and fade-outs. Smooth out the very beginning and the very end of a sound file. Reversing sounds: Reverse all or a portion of a digital audio recording

Delivery

To play sound on a computer system, a sound card and speakers, or a headset are needed. The digital audio file is sent through a digital-to-analog converter **(DAC)** so that it can be heard. It is important to test sounds under a variety of different conditions.

Using human speech as an input device is called voice recognition.

Using the computer to articulate human speech is called speech synthesis.

A device that is either software or hardware for recording sound is called a sequencer.

Monophonic vs. Stereo Sound

Monophonic sounds: flat and unrealistic when compared to stereo sounds. Stereo sounds: much more dynamic and life like. Monophonic sound files are sometimes a more appropriate choice where storage and transfer time are major concerns. Narration and voiceovers can effectively be saved in a monophonic format. Music almost always must be recorded and saved in stereo.

It is recommended that videos should be prepared in 1280x720p and using the H.264 video codec at about 4000kb/s. As a general rule, this compression rate will be suitable for video to be displayed on most smartphones, tablets and computers.

There are two types editing that we use to edit videos, one is linear editing and other is non-linear editing.

Linear editing - Linear editing was the method originally used with analogue video tapes.

Non-Linear editing - Non-linear video editing is achieved by loading the video material into a computer from analogue or digital tape.

Competency 009: The Technology Applications teacher knows how to design, produce and distribute multimedia products.

Bandwidth is the speed that you can send data or receive the data. It depends upon the bit rate at which the data is send or received. For more bit rate the bandwidth consumed is more for which the cost to broadcaster will increase. As the bit rate increases the amount of data streamed per second increases at a good sampling rate to produce the replica of analog signal with more bit depth (16 for audio) thus increasing the bandwidth and file size to produce the best audio quality. Some of the bit rate and sample rate preferred are given below: For MP3format the Mp3 streaming bit rates and sample rate for stereo may range from 96–320 kbps/44.1–48KHz, the preferred bit rates are 128Kbps/44.1KHz, 96Kbps/44.1KHz. The audio quality depends on the encoded format, it is difficult to determine which encoded format at chosen bit rate sounds good. For example the bit rate at 128kbps Mp3 format sounds the same quality as AAC format at 96kbps/44.1KHz(apple lossy compressed format for iTunes).

Bit Rate calculation (Uncompressed Format) bit rate=bits per sample (16-bit or 24-bit) *samples per sec (44.1KHz-48KHz) *number of channels. Example 16-bit 48Khz stereo contains bitrate of 1.5Mb/sec. File size calculation For Uncompressed Format file size= (bits per sample (16-bit or 24-bit)*samples per sec ((44.1KHz-48KHz)*number of channels*duration(number of sec the music played))/8. Example 16-bit 44.1Khz stereo for 60 min the file size is 630MB. For Compressed Format File size=((bit rate in kbps)*(length of the audio in sec))/8 Example 16 bit 44.1Khz stereo for 60min at 128Kbps the file size is 10.8MB For live streaming the bandwidth required can be calculated using the formula: bandwidth=listeners*bit rate*length(audio length per day)*no. of days. The bandwidth required for bit rate of 128Kbps is 57.6MB/hr. Table Representing the bandwidth for various Bitrates The length of the file is taken as 60min (180 sec)

A portfolio is a compilation of files or work samples documenting the students' academic activities and accomplishments. Portfolios can take several forms, and the format you choose depends on the purpose of your portfolio and how you plan to use it.

A traditional portfolio is maintained in a printed format with hard copies of the student(s) work carefully organized and presented in a three-ring binder or coil binding.

An online portfolio contains electronic copies of the student work but keep in mind confidentiality and safety by making sure the portfolio is on the school server. The file types/formats can vary depending on the type of information that is being shared. For example, this could include pdf files, html files, hyperlinks, audio files, and video files. The online portfolio adds versatility by enabling the ability to share their work to parents via the school website.

Ethics of Electronic Publishing

Quality is closely related to the ethical principle of "do no harm" and to the virtues of honesty and integrity.

Security is closely related to the ethical tenets of privacy and confidentiality.

Access is related to the ethical principle of justice. Justice can be defined as fairness or as giving person(s), group(s), or society(ies) what is due or owed them.

Domain IV — Web Design

Competency 010: The Technology Applications teacher demonstrates knowledge of strategies and techniques for website administration.

What is Internet?

The Internet is essentially a global network of computing resources. The Internet is pretty much a physical collection of routers and circuits as a set of shared resources.

Some common definitions that were given in the past include –

A network of networks based on the TCP/IP communications protocol.

A community of people who use and develop those networks.

A community of people who use and develop those networks.

Internet-Based Services

Some of the basic services available to Internet users are

Email – A fast, easy, and inexpensive way to communicate with other Internet users around the world.

Telnet – Allows a user to log into a remote computer as though it were a local system.

FTP – Allows a user to transfer virtually every kind of file that can be stored on a computer from one Internet-connected computer to another.

UseNet news – A distributed bulletin board that offers a combination news and discussion service on thousands of topics.

World Wide Web (WWW) – A hypertext interface to Internet information resources.

What is WWW?

WWW acronym means World Wide Web. A technical definition of the World Wide Web is – All the resources and users on the Internet that are using the Hypertext Transfer Protocol **(HTTP).**

A broader definition comes from the organization that Web inventor Tim Berners-Lee helped found, the World Wide Web Consortium (W3C): The World Wide Web is the universe of network-accessible information, an embodiment of human knowledge.

In simple terms, The World Wide Web is a way of exchanging information between computers on the Internet, tying them together into a vast collection of interactive multimedia resources.

What is HTTP?

HTTP stands for Hypertext Transfer Protocol. This is the protocol being used to transfer hypertext documents that makes the World Wide Web possible.

A standard web address such as Yahoo.com is called a URL and here the prefix http indicates its protocol.

What is URL?

URL stands for Uniform Resource Locator and is used to specify addresses on the World Wide Web. A URL is the fundamental network identification for any resource connected to the web (e.g., hypertext pages, images, and sound files).

A URL will have the following format –protocol://hostname/other information

The protocol specifies how information is transferred from a link. The protocol used for web resources is HyperText Transfer Protocol (HTTP). Other protocols compatible with most web browsers include FTP, telnet, newsgroups, and Gopher.

The protocol is followed by a colon, two slashes, and then the domain name. The domain name is the computer on which the resource is located.

Links to particular files or subdirectories may be further specified after the domain name. The directory names are separated by single forward slashes.

What is a Website?

Website is a collection of various pages written in HTML markup language. This is a location on the web where people can find tutorials on latest technologies. Similarly, there are millions of websites available on the web.

Each page available on the website is called a web page and first page of any website is called

65

home page for that site.

What is Web Server?

Every Website sits on a computer known as a Web server. This server is always connected to the internet. Every Web server that is connected to the Internet is given a unique address made up of a series of four numbers between 0 and 256 separated by periods. For example, 68.178.157.132 or 68.122.35.127.

When registering a Web address, also known as a domain name, such as passtexes.com it must specify the IP address of the Web server that will host the site.

What is Web Browser?

Web Browsers are software installed on your PC. In order to access the Web, a web browser such as Microsoft Internet Explorer, BING, Google Chrome or Mozilla Firefox.

What is SMTP Server?

SMTP stands for Simple Mail Transfer Protocol Server. This server takes care of delivering emails from one server to another server. When a person sends an email to another email address, it is delivered to its recipient by a SMTP Server.

What is ISP?

ISP stands for Internet Service Provider. This is companies that provide service in terms of internet connection to connect to the internet.

What is HTML?

HTML stands for Hyper Text Markup Language. This is the language in which web pages are written to build a website.

What is Hyperlink?

A hyperlink or simply a link is a selectable element in an electronic document that serves as an access point to other electronic resources. Familiar hyperlinks include buttons, icons, image maps, and clickable text links.

What is DNS?

DNS stands for Domain Name System. When someone types in your domain name, www.example.com, your browser will ask the Domain Name System to find the IP that hosts your site. When you register your domain name, your IP address should be put in a DNS along with your domain name. Without doing it your domain name will not be functioning properly.

What is W3C?

W3C stands for World Wide Web Consortium which is an international consortium of companies involved with the Internet and the Web.

The W3C was founded in 1994 by Tim Berners-Lee, the original architect of the World Wide Web. The organization's purpose is to develop open standards so that the Web evolves in a single direction rather than being splintered among competing factions. The W3C is the chief standards body for HTTP and HTML.

Web physically consists of the following components −

Your personal computer − A Web browser −An internet connection − A Web server - Routers & Switches.

The Web is known as a client-server system. The computer is the client and the remote computers that store electronic files are the servers. A user enters a URL into a browser (for example, http://tx.nesinc.com. This request is passed to a domain name server.

The domain name server returns an IP address for the server that hosts the Website (for example, 68.178.157.132).

The browser requests the page from the Web server using the IP address specified by the domain name server.

The Web server returns the page to the IP address specified by the browser requesting the page. The page may also contain links to other files on the same server, such as images, which the browser will also request.

The browser collects all the information and displays to your computer in the form of Web page.

List of Steps to Build a Website

1. Computer – it should have Windows or Linux or UNIX or Macintosh system or any other operating system.

2. Internet Connection

3. Web Server

4. Text Editor – this is used to write HTML, PHP or ASP pages or for any other editing purpose. Or Web Authoring Tools – instead of a simple Text Editor to edit HTML files then there are many commercial Web Authoring Tools available. These tools are also

called HTML editors. Microsoft's FrontPage and Macromedia Dreamweaver are both a visual HTML (WYSIWYG --- What You See Is What You Get) and HTML source code editor. These editors help develop HTML pages quickly.

5. Web Browser – this will allow to view the website.

Secure FTP client - An SFTP client is a software which uses the SFTP protocol to transfer files securely to and from a remote computer.

Secure Shell SSH – A SSH client is a software which uses the SSH protocol to connect to a remote computer. In general, SSH protocol can be used for two purposes, file transfers and terminal access.

Gopher is a protocol designed to search, retrieve, and display documents from remote sites on the Internet. In addition to document display, document retrieval, it is possible to initiate on-line connections with other systems via Gopher. Information accessible via Gopher is stored on many computers all over the Internet called Gopher servers.

WAIS (Wide Area Information Server) is an Internet search tool that has the capability of searching many databases at one time. The databases to be searched can be determined by the user. When WAIS completes a search, it is actually searching an index of the database.

A domain name is the part of your Internet address that comes after "www".

.edu - Register a domain name for education purpose.
.com – Stands for company/commercial, but it can be used for any website.
.net – Stands for network and is usually used for a network of sites.
.org – Stands for organization and is supposed to be for non-profit bodies.
.us, .in – They are based on your country names so that you can go for country specific domain extensions.
.biz – A newer extension on the Internet and can be used to indicate that this site is purely related to business.
.info – Stands for information. This domain name extension can be very useful, and as a newcomer it's doing well.
.tv – Stands for Television and are more appropriate for TV channel sites.
.mil - Stands for military it is used for the armed forces.

ICANN

Internet Corporation for Assigned Names and Numbers is responsible for managing domain name distribution and administration. Helping to set standards for the purchasing, transferring, and other processes relating to domain names, this organization is commissioned with the task of serving the world's needs independent of governments.

Internet: Millions of computer systems are interconnected for sharing information across the globe. Anyone can access it for downloading and uploading files. Internet subscribers are increasing day by day at an exponential rate.

Intranet: It is really simple in which network exists in some company, school, and Government offices premises and have list of authorized users who can access particular information in the form or files, folders. Everyone cannot use Intranet, and it has very limited connectivity.

Network security is any activity designed to protect the usability and integrity of a network and its data. It includes the hardware and software technologies. Network security effectively manages access to the network. It targets a variety of threats and stops them from entering or spreading on your network.

Types of network security

- **Access control**
- **Not every user should have access to your network.**
- **Antivirus and antimalware software**
- **"Malware," short for "malicious software," includes viruses, worms, Trojans, ransomware, and spyware.**
- **Application security**
- **Any software used needs to be protected**
    - **Email security**
    - **Email gateways are the number one threat vector for a security breach.**
    - **Firewalls**
    - **Firewalls put up a barrier between your trusted internal network and untrusted outside networks, such as the Internet.**

VPN

A virtual private network encrypts the connection from an endpoint to a network, often over the Internet.

Bandwidth: the level of traffic, and amount of data that can transfer between a site, users, and the Internet. The more bandwidth a data connection has, the more data it can send and receive at one time. Bandwidth can be compared to the amount of water that can flow through a water pipe. The bigger the pipe, the more water can flow through it at one time. Bandwidth works on the same principle. So, the higher the capacity of the communication link, or pipe, the more data can flow through it per second. End users pay for the capacity of their network connections, so the greater the capacity of the link, the more expensive it is.

Competency 011: The Technology Applications teacher knows principles of Web design and implements a variety of tools and techniques to create and troubleshoot Web pages for a diverse audience.

Under Competency 011 Gaming content questions were asked so this information is included in this section.

Computer game or a PC game is played on a PC

Console game is played on a device specifically designed for gaming

Video game has evolved into a catchall phrase that encompasses the above along with any game made for mobile phones, tablets, etc.

Games are often classified into genres, which purport to define games in terms of having a common style or set of characteristics.

Adventure games

- Typically, the player is the protagonist of a story and in order to progress must solve puzzles. The puzzles can often involve manipulating and interacting with in-game objects, characters, etc.
- Text-based adventures and graphical
- Examples:
– Zork
– King's Quest

Action games

- Several other action-oriented genres can be broadly classified as belonging to this genre. Action games are typified by fast-paced events and movement which often have to be performed reflexively.
- Games such as Pong and Space Invaders initially defined the genre.

Action-adventure games

- Action-adventure games can be described in terms of a blend of the characteristics associated with both adventure and action games, i.e. often involving both exploration and puzzle solving alongside fast-paced action sequences.

notable examples include:
Legend of Zelda

Platform games aka platformers

- This genre often requires the protagonist to run and jump between surfaces (i.e. platforms) whilst avoiding game objects and the detrimental effects of gravity.
- Traditionally, platform games were side-on 2D in perspective and very popular on earlier gaming platforms.
- The genre has declined in popularity in recent years, although some titles have successfully redefined the genre to include 3D environments.
- Examples:
  – Super Mario Bros
  – Sonic the Hedgehog
  – Super Mario 64
  – Tomb Raider
  – Prince of Persia

Fighting games

- In fighting games, the player typically fights other players or

the computer in some form of one-on-one combat.
- Examples:
  - Tekken
  - Mortal Kombat
  - Street Fighter

First-person shooter (FPS) games

- Action games where the player is "behind the eyes" of the game character in a first-person perspective. Although a number of FPS games also support third-person views.
- Most FPSs are fast-paced and typically require actions to be performed reflexively.
- Notable examples include:
  - DOOM
  - Half-Life
  - Far Cry

Real-time strategy (RTS) games

- RTS games typically defined several goals around resource collection, base and unit construction and engagement in combat with other players or computer opponents who also share similar goals.
- Emphasis is often placed upon managing logistics, resources and production.
- Notable examples include:
  - Warcraft
  - Age of Empires

Role playing games (RPGs)

- Originally started out as video games based on pen and pencil games like Dungeons and Dragons. A fantasy theme is often retained.
- Often characterized in terms of providing the player with flexibility in terms of character development, problem resolution, etc.
- Notable examples include:
  - Final Fantasy

Massively multiplayer online role-playing games (MMRPGs)

• Typically, an RPG set in a persistent virtual world populated by thousands of other players. MMORPGs can be viewed as evolving from text-based MUDs in mid-to-late 1990s.
• The first highly popular MMORPG was Ultima Online whilst World of Warcraft holds the honor of being the current most popular.
Simulation games
• Many simulation games aim to simulate physical activities such as flying an aircraft (Microsoft Flight Simulator), playing golf or football etc. (sometimes with as much realism as possible).
• Other forms of simulation game aim to provide simulations of forms of management, e.g. football management games, city management (SimCity), railroading, etc.

Racing games

• Racing games typically place the player behind the wheel and involve competing in a race against other drivers and/or time. Two sub-genres can be identified: simulation and arcade.
• Examples include:
– Pole Position
– Mario Kart
– Gran Turismo
– Need for Speed
– GTR

The Four Basic Principles of Graphic Design

Author Robin Williams written a book that is extremely popular the title Non-Designers

Design Book, she stated there are four principles of design that underlie every design project:

- **Alignment**
- **Proximity**
- **Contrast**
- **Repetition**

Alignment refers to how text and graphics are placed on the page. It creates order, organizes page elements, indicates groups of items, and emphasizes visual connection. There are two basic types of alignment: edge and center. Edges can be aligned along the top, bottom left or right. Center alignment can be either horizontal or vertical. When designing a page, be sure that each element (text, graphics, photographs) has a visual alignment with another item.

Proximity describes the distance between individual design elements. Proximity implies a relationship between the elements; conversely, lack of proximity separates them. Like alignment, proximity is a tool of visual organization. Placing elements in close proximity unifies them and communicates a sense of order and organization to the reader. When it isn't possible to group items proximately, then unity between two elements can be achieved by using a third element to connect them.

Contrast adds interest as well as organization to the page and is created when two elements are different. Common ways to create contrast include varying size, color, thickness, shape, style or space. The greater the difference between elements, the greater the contrast. Besides adding interest to the page, contrast can be used to direct the reader around the page and to emphasize importance or differences. Contrast is only effective when it is evident.

Repetition brings visual consistency to page design. When the same design elements—such as uniform size and weight of headline fonts or use of initial caps to begin a chapter—are used, it becomes clear that the pages are related to each other part of the same document. In this way, repetition creates unity. Some examples of repetition are using the same style of headlines, the same style of initial capitals, or repeating the same basic layout from one page to another.

The four principles of design are interconnected and work together to communicate the message. Contrast is often the most important visual attraction on a page. If the page elements are not the same, then make them very different instead of making them similar. Repetition helps develop the organization and strengthens the unity of a page. Repeating visual elements develops the design. Every element should have some visual connection

with another element on the page, creating a consistent and sophisticated alignment.

The Basis of Good Design

Author Chuck Green discusses the basis of good design in his book The Desktop Publisher's Idea Book, he describes the five steps:

- Set the goal
- Compose the message
- Choose the medium
- Select a design
- Illustrate the message

Set the goal

Every design task begins by defining the end to be achieved—the goal of the design project, which is most often related to the action desired by the target audience. Is the purpose to invite an inquiry? Is it to generate a purchase? Would it persuade the reader to a new point of view? Keep the goal in mind and allow it to determine the design.

Compose the message

The message is the most important element of any marketing piece—it informs the reader of the benefits of taking action Affecting behavior is the result of explaining to the reader what to expect from the product or service . . . "What's in it for me?"

Choose the medium

The project's purpose and message both determine the layout. Sometimes the layout will be obvious—a business card or a display ad. Other times the choices will be broader—a flyer, brochure, or self-mailer. The ultimate choice might be determined by the method of delivery to the target audience (e.g., direct mail, trade show, or mailed in response to an inquiry).

Select a design

To achieve maximum effectiveness, a design must take into account a myriad of elements related to the target audience (e.g. age, education, language skills, visual preferences, cultural expectations, level of knowledge, and desires). These and other factors affect the selection of color palette, fonts, illustrations, and photographs. Illustrate the message utilizing photographs and illustrations.

- **Be sparse and simple.**
- **Use color sparingly.**
- **Limit the selection of fonts.**
- **Write clear, comprehensible copy.**

Static Website and Dynamic Website

Websites that only use HTML and CSS are called static websites, and websites with scripting are called dynamic websites.

A Static Website

A static website is the simplest kind of website you can build. Static websites are written in HTML and CSS only, with no scripting. The only form of interactivity on a static website is hyperlinks.

A Dynamic Website

A dynamic website is a website that not only uses HTML and CSS but includes website scripting as well. There are two main reasons why you'd want to use website scripting on your site: you want an interactive web app that people can use, not just read you want to be able to share HTML code between your pages.

Basic Web Design

Design a website using hand code which is programming in HTML, utilizing a text editor like notepad or use WYSIWYG (What You See Is What You Get)This is the term used to describe the HTML editors that give you a graphical representation of what you're coding.

HTML, CSS, and JavaScript are three district coding languages that together are used to build Website and Web Applications.

HTML: Hyper-Text Markup Language is used to put the structure of a website together. (Like a skeleton of a body)

CSS: Cascading Style Sheets acts like makeup for the HTML. CSS improves the colors and layout of a website structure built with HTML.

JavaScript is a full-on programming language that adds interactivity and functionality to a website.

HTML is the standard markup language for creating Web pages. HTML stands for Hyper Text Markup Language. HTML describes the structure of Web pages using markup. HTML elements are the building blocks of HTML pages. HTML elements are represented by tags. HTML tags label pieces of content such as "heading", "paragraph", "table", and so on. **Browsers do not display the HTML tags, but use them to render the content of the page example below:**

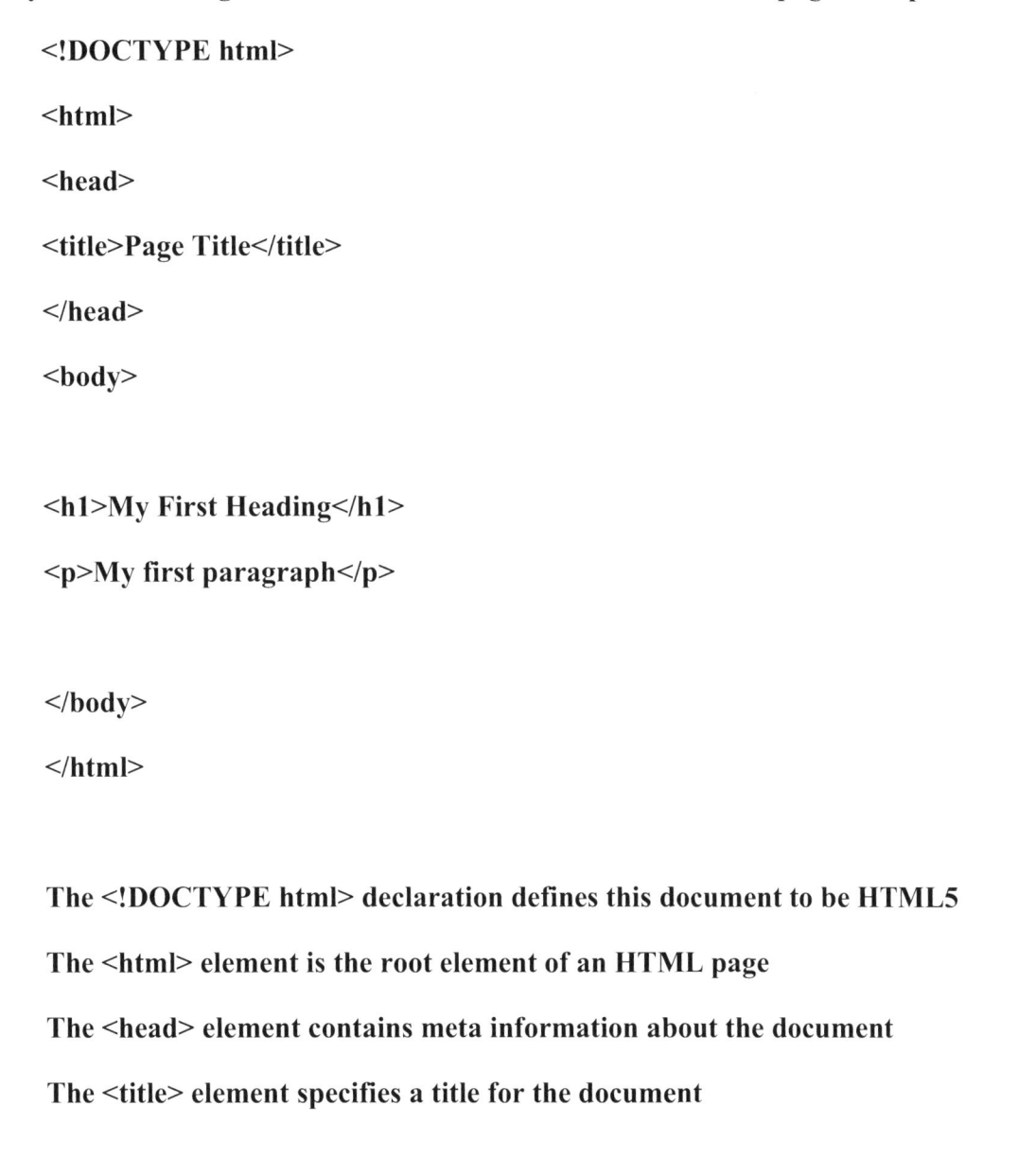

```
<!DOCTYPE html>
<html>
<head>
<title>Page Title</title>
</head>
<body>


<h1>My First Heading</h1>
<p>My first paragraph</p>


</body>
</html>
```

The <!DOCTYPE html> declaration defines this document to be HTML5

The <html> element is the root element of an HTML page

The <head> element contains meta information about the document

The <title> element specifies a title for the document

The <body> element contains the visible page content

The <h1> element defines a large heading

The <p> element defines a paragraph

The <br> element with no contents defines line break

HTML Tags

HTML tags are element names surrounded by angle brackets:

<tagname>content goes here...</tagname>

HTML tags normally come in pairs like <p> and </p>

The first tag in a pair is the start tag, the second tag is the end tag

The end tag is written like the start tag, but with a forward slash inserted before the tag name

Competency 012: The Technology Applications teacher knows how to use Web pages to communicate and interact effectively with others.

Accessibility Principles W3C Web Accessibility Initiative

Web accessibility basically means that people with disabilities can use the Web. More specifically, web accessibility means that people with disabilities can perceive, understand, navigate, and interact with the Web.

Captions for audio: Captions are text describing sound in video or audio, such as people speaking and other important sounds. Captions are vital for people who are deaf.

Device independence: Websites should be designed so that they don't require a specific type of device, such as a mouse. This also helps "power users" who are faster with keyboard shortcuts, people needing to limit mouse use due to repetitive stress injuries (RSI), and people using mobile phones and other devices without a mouse.

Clear and consistent design and navigation: People with some kinds of cognitive disabilities have difficulty processing visual information. Clear and consistent design and navigation also benefit people who magnify web pages significantly and people with "tunnel vision" who see only a small part of the web page at a time.

Online Etiquette - Netiquette

Remember the human, be friendly - Before writing a post or response, ask yourself, "Would I say this to a person face to face?" If the answer is no, do not post or send it. There is a human being on the other side of the computer screen.

Adhere to same standards of behavior online that you follow in real-life - When you are in your room in front of your computer, the law seems far away. Be ethical. Remember breaking the law is horribly bad netiquette.

Avoid using all caps - (IT'S LIKE SHOUTING!) You should only capitalize individual words in a sentence to highlight or emphasize a point, not an entire sentence or paragraph.

Avoid responding when emotions are high - If you are angry or have a strong opinion about something someone has written/posted, wait to reply until after you have calmed down. Writing to express a strong opinion is "flaming" and can lead to "flaming wars". No one wins those wars. Don't feed the flames; extinguish them by guiding the discussion back to a more productive direction.

Respect the privacy of others - Do not forward emails without permission or copy discussions or chat dialog and post publicly. Before you send an email, make sure you have correctly addressed it to the intended recipient. Good rule of thumb is if you forward someone else's email, include the person who wrote the original email in cc of the forward.

Respect intellectual property of others - Be ethical, academically honest, and follow copyright laws. Cite ideas and quotes that you have used from other people.

Make yourself look good - Post intelligent messages despite the informality of the conversation. Avoid posting messages with grammatical, spelling, and typographical errors.

Be forgiving of other people's mistakes - Remember everyone at one time was new to online. Be gentle with those that might make mistakes. Blasting out all the errors in grammar, spelling, or sentence structure is often troubling for someone who does not take criticism well. Private corrections are the responsibility of the instructor.

Texting & Abbreviations - Texting has a place, and it is not in an online course. It is probably safe to use emoticons and abbreviations in chatting but not messages or emails. Suggestion - follow the instructor's lead. Does the instructor use emoticons? Does the instructor use common abbreviations and acronyms such as FYI, BTW, IMO, LOL? Not sure? Ask the Teacher.

Know where you are in cyberspace - Netiquette varies from domain to domain. For example, an online course may have a gaming environment or a virtual world simulation. What may be appropriate in one place, may not be appropriate in another. Get a sense of how other people act, then go ahead and participate.

Impact of Technology

Technological Globalization is impacted in large part by technological diffusion, the spread of technology across borders. Technological Social Control and Digital Surveillance, digital security cameras capture our movements, observers can track us through our cell phones, and police forces around the world use facial-recognition software

Media and technology have been intermingled from the beginning of human communication. The printing press, the telegraph, and the internet are all examples of their intersection. Mass media has allowed for more shared social experiences, but new media now creates a seemingly endless amount of airtime for any and every voice that wants to be heard. Advertising has also changed with technology. New media allows consumers to bypass traditional advertising venues, causing companies to be more innovative and intrusive as they try to gain everyone's attention.

DOMAIN I REVIEW QUESTIONS

Questions for Domain 1

1. An assessment of a project or activity after the student has completed the work. This will identify if the student has met the learning objectives and satisfied the requirements of the project.

    a) Rubric

    b) Formal

    c) Summative

    d) Augmentative

2. First software loaded on a computer. It manages all the software applications and determines which applications take priority, manages memory requests, and communicates with input and output devices. (Example: Linux, Windows XP, and Macintosh X.)

    a) Applications

    b) Operating Systems

    c) Authoring Systems

    d) Boot INI

3. Holds all content for a particular subject, year or grade level. It also tracks student progress for teachers. It can use combinations of drill and practice, tutorials, simulation, and problem-solving software. The instruction is highly individualized for each student.

    a) Project Management Tools

    b) Spreadsheets

    c) Database

    d) Word Processor

4. Allows the computer to process the data, sometimes call the brain.

    a) CPU

    b) Hard Drive

    c) RAM

    d) Motherboard

5. A connector for a device that sends or receives several bits of data simultaneously by using more than one wire.

    a) Firewire

    b) USB

    c) Parallel port

    d) HDMI

6. Which memory is considered volatile?

    a) SDRAM

    b) ROM

    c) DRAM

    d) RAM

7. What program use a mathematical formula to display and scale the image without distortion?

   a) Raster

   b) Graphic Interface

   c) Vector

   d) Bitmap

8. Which typically describes the network used by a local school district?

   a) WAN

   b) LAN

   c) Intranet

   d) MAN

9. The System in finding information on the internet

   a) Server

   b) GOPHER

   c) Routing

   d) FTP

10. The computer language that uses string of numbers

   a) Binary

   b) Coding

   c) HTML

   d) C++

DOMAIN II REVIEW QUESTIONS

Domain 2 Questions

1. The pictures and texts have jagged edges, what process should be used to smooth out the edges?

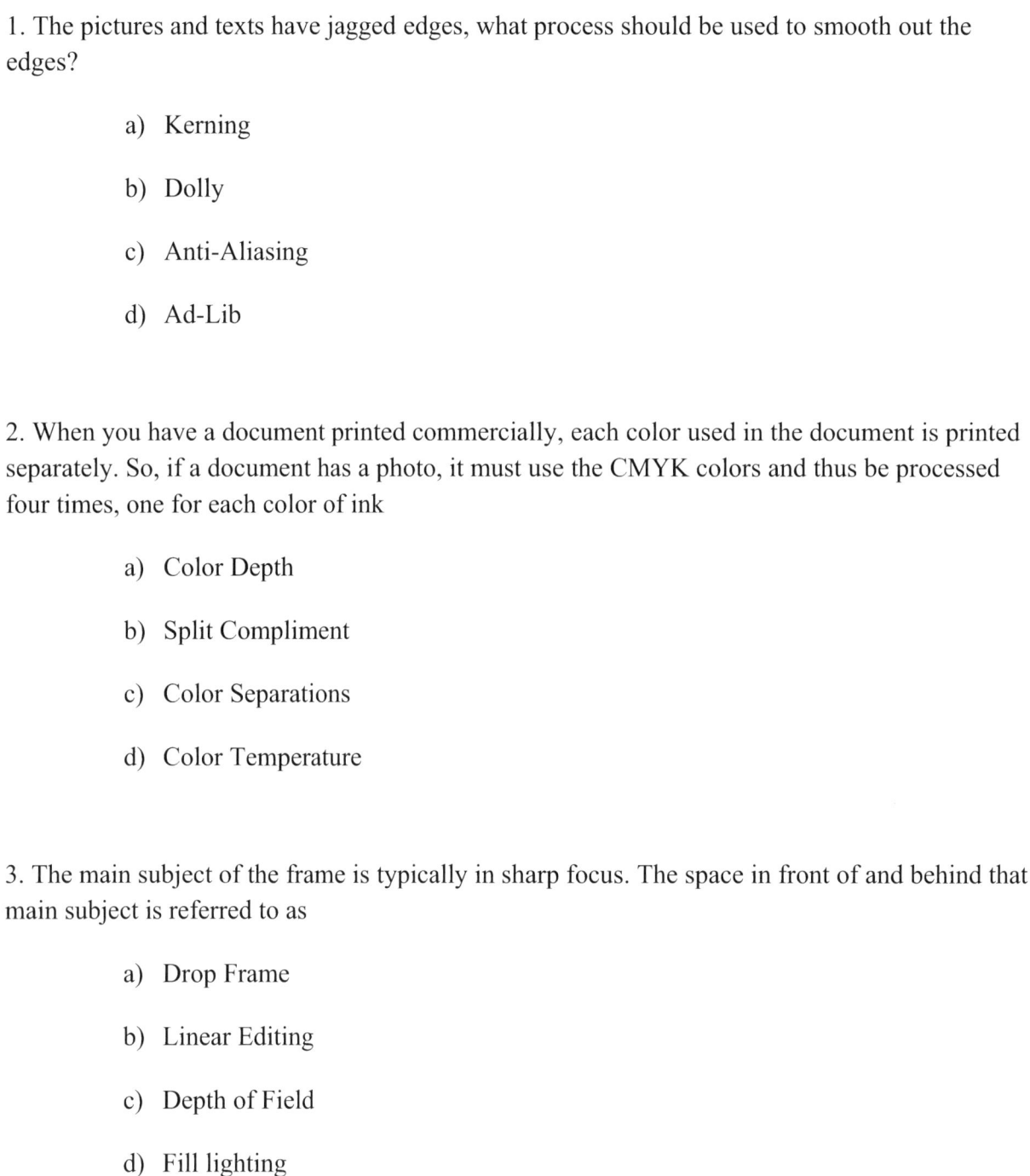

    a) Kerning

    b) Dolly

    c) Anti-Aliasing

    d) Ad-Lib

2. When you have a document printed commercially, each color used in the document is printed separately. So, if a document has a photo, it must use the CMYK colors and thus be processed four times, one for each color of ink

    a) Color Depth

    b) Split Compliment

    c) Color Separations

    d) Color Temperature

3. The main subject of the frame is typically in sharp focus. The space in front of and behind that main subject is referred to as

    a) Drop Frame

    b) Linear Editing

    c) Depth of Field

    d) Fill lighting

4. Runs the camera, taking directions from the Director.

    a) Executive Producer

    b) Gopher

    c) Camera Operator

    d) Boomer

5. The camera sweeps in movement but it is up and down rather than side to side.

    a) Pan

    b) Tilt

    c) Bird's Eye

    d) Back Light

6. What is the compression format for QuickTime movies?

    a) AVI

    b) WAV

    c) MOV

    d) MPEG4

7. 3D modeling technique in which the artist begins with a low-resolution primitive (typically a cube or sphere) and modifies the shape by extruding, scaling, or rotating faces and edges.

    a) Rendering

    b) Rotoscoping

    c) Box 3D

    d) Morphing

8. The number of bits used to represent a color.

    a) Color Depth

    b) CODEC

    c) Contrast

    d) Bitmap

9. In animation programs, you can set two keyframes at the beginning and the end of a certain motion.

    a) Tweening

    b) Collation

    c) Kerning

    d) Typefaces

10. It is typically used for photographs displayed on web pages because it can display 16 million colors, but it compresses images to take up less memory. It compresses images by actually throwing out some of the subtle color changes.

   a) PNG

   b) BMP

   c) JPEG

   d) Vector

DOMAIN III REVIEW QUESTIONS

Domain 3 Questions

1. Designed to illuminate the subject, not the background. It is placed above and behind the actors or subject.

   a) Back Light

   b) Fill Light

   c) Contrast Light

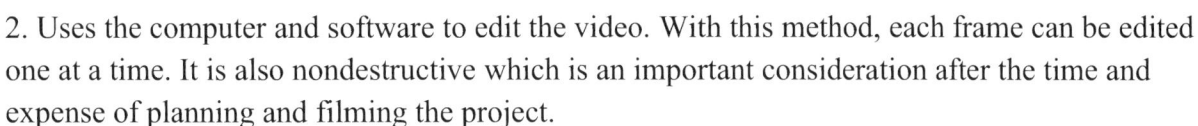

   d) Spot Light

2. Uses the computer and software to edit the video. With this method, each frame can be edited one at a time. It is also nondestructive which is an important consideration after the time and expense of planning and filming the project.

   a) Editor

   b) Assistant Editor

   c) Linear Editing

   d) Non-linear Editing

3. Files can be much smaller than other compression schemes and still retain quality.

   a) PNG

   b) MOV

   c) JPEG

   d) SWF

4. Opening in a lens which allows light to pass through is also known as the iris

    a) Aperture

    b) Long Shot

    c) Frame

    d) Analog

5. Written before filming starts.

    a) Script

    b) Storyboard

    c) Dialogue

    d) Ad-lib

6. Camera shot were person appears small

    a) Long shot

    b) Tilt

    c) Worm view

    d) Extra-long shot

7. Coordinates and schedules the people and equipment necessary for the production.

    a) Director

    b) Engineer

    c) Producer

    d) Screenwriter

8. It translates signals or transmissions from analog to digital or from digital to analog.

    a) Network protocol

    b) Scanner

    c) CODEC

    d) Router

9. The musical component of the multimedia product.

    a) Score

    b) Symphony

    c) Music data

    d) Orchestra

10. The compression format for QuickTime movies.

    a) AVI

    b) iTunes

    c) MPEG4

    d) MOV

DOMAIN IV REVIEW QUESTIONS

DOMAIN 4 Questions

1. A computer network that spans a wider area than a local area network

    a) Intranet

    b) LAN

    c) WAN

    d) MAN

2. A clickable link that takes you from one document to another, or to any resource, even within the same document, with text that is highlighted is called

    a) Locator

    b) Url

    c) Hyperlink

    d) Protocol

3. What is a CMS in web design

    a) Content Management System

    b) Creative Management System

    c) Content Mixing System

    d) Creatives Managerial System

4. HTML document start and end with which tag pairs?

    a. <HEAD>....</HEAD>

    b. <BODY>....</BODY>

    c. <HTML>....</HTML>

    d. <WEB>....</WEB>

5. What does the .com domain represents?

    a) Education domain

    b) Commercial domain

    c) Network

    d) None of the above

6. Typing in all capitals in electronic communications means:

    a) this message is very important.

    b) you are shouting.

    c) it's okay to forward this message to others.

    d) nothing special--typing in all caps is normal.

7. Consists of one or more web pages that relate to a common theme such as person, business, organization, or subject

    a) hit

    b) network

    c) back

    d) website

8. Worldwide network of interconnected computers

   a) Average

   b) CTRL A

   c) Internet

   d) ARPANET

9. Computer jargon, WWW stands for

   a) worldwide web
   b) worldwide wildlife
   c) worldwide women's
   d) worldwide week

10. A company-wide network, closed to public access, which uses Internet-type technology is called:

   a) Internet

   b) Intranet

   c) Extranet

   d) All of the above

DOMAIN I - IV REVIEW ANSWERS

DOMAIN I	DOMAIN II	DOMAIN III	DOMAIN IV
1. C	1. C	1. D	1. D
2. B	2. C	2. A	2. B
3. C	3. C	3. C	3. A
4. A	4. C	4. A	4. C
5. C	5. B	5. A	5. B
6. D	6. C	6. D	6. B
7. C	7. C	7. C	7. D
8. C	8. A	8. C	8. C
9. D	9. A	9. A	9. A
10. D	10. C	10. D	10. B

PRACTIVE EXAM QUESTIONS

1. Popular with photographers. It divides their view into thirds horizontally and vertically. Photographers try to place focal point on the grid rather than center of picture.

   a) camera's point of view

   b) golden mean

   c) golden ratio

   d) rule of thirds

2. What is the best way to grade a technology portfolio project?

   a) rubric

   b) self-assessment

   c) presentation

   d) discussion boards

3. A Teacher was informed about a new educational software to use for class, what four points to look for when evaluating software?

   a) cost, brand, quality, age appropriate

   b) brand, style, effective, quality

   c) age appropriate, quality, effective, efficient

   d) cost, age appropriate, effective, efficient

4. Also known as raster graphic. Format is created from pixels or small dots of color; it is also known as a raster graphic.

   a) bitmap

   b) GIF

   c) MPEG4

   d) vector

5. Most of the time this font is used with prints it has a small line that is used for decorative purposes on letters.

   a) kerning

   b) sans serif

   c) Arial

   d) serif

6. What colors that make you feel comfort, energy, excitement and sometimes anger?

   a) warm colors

   b) cool colors

   c) primary colors

   d) secondary colors

7. Is the secure form of http the connection is encrypted.

   a) HTTP

   b) FTP

   c) HTTPS

   d) TC/IP

8. On the color wheel it has three colors. one color and two colors that are next to each other. Ex: green, red-orange.

   a) color compliment

   b) secondary colors

   c) split compliment

   d) primary colors

9. Known as universal colors there are 256 colors that all monitors support.

   a) color scheme

   b) web safe colors

   c) warm colors

   d) triad colors

10. What manages all the software applications including which applications takes priority, as well as, manages memory, communicates with input and output devices.

    a) Operating System

    b) Boot INI

    c) Authority Software

    d) CPU

11. It is the space in front and behind the focused subject.

    a) panning

    b) depth field

    c) drop frame

    d) background shot

12. Software process were object is changed into another object

    a) rendering

    b) rotoscope

    c) morphing

    d) tweening

13. What camera shot were the lens move in closer and the camera stays in one place?

    a) extra-long shot

    b) zoom

    c) birds' eye

    d) up close

14. Camera view moves slow and smooth while making sweeping movement from side to side.

    a) long shot

    b) overview

    c) body shot

    d) pan

15. It is a type of frame the is used in major parts of an animation were change in a timeline, it is also important for tweening.

    a) expediate frame

    b) key frame

    c) frame-to-frame

    d) frames

16. It performs a specific task for the end user. Ex: word processing, spreadsheets

    a) System

    b) Software

    c) Program

    d) Application

17. An IP address is a _____ number.

   a) 16 bit

   b) 32 bit

   c) 8 bit

   d) 64 bit

18. A person who sends irrelevant or unsolicited messages by using Internet, usually to large numbers of users, for the purposes of advertising, spreading malware, phishing, etc. is known as

   a) Spammer

   b) Hacker

   c) Anonymous

   d) none of the above

19. The Windows 10 operating system uses a GUI, which stands for:

   a) guided user interaction

   b) graphical user interface

   c) graphics utility interface.

   d) graphical utility interaction.

20. The only language which the computer understands is _____

   a) Assembly Language

   b) Binary Language

   c) BASIC

   d) C Language

21. Saving data and instructions to make them readily available is the job of _____

a) Storage Unit

b) Cache Unit

c) Input Unit

d) Output Unit

22. The two basic types of memory in a computer are _____

a) Primary and major

b) Primary and Secondary

c) Minor and Major

d) Main and virtual

23. Expansion of FTP is

a) Fine Transfer Protocol

b) File Transfer Protocol

c) First Transfer Protocol

d) None of the mentioned

24. FTP is built on _____ architecture

a) Client-server

b) P2P

c) Both of the above

d) None of the above

25. What does a document show when a design consistently uses the same typeface for headings, subheadings, captions, and text?

   a) A Rhythm

   b) B Emphasis

   c) C Unity

   d) D Shape

26. What is Desktop Publishing?

   a) An application software like PageMaker

   b) The use of audio editing equipment

   c) The use of a computer system and graphic software

   d) A software that allows you to layout a document

27. Empty space in a design is often referred to as:

   a) White space

   b) Area.

   c) Foreground.

   d) Background

28. What is the visual perception of motion that is repetitive?

   a) Contrast

   b) Movement

   c) Emphasis

   d) Rhythm

29. _____ line, shape, form, color, value, space and texture

   a) Color temperature

   b) The Element of Art

   c) The components of color

   d) Art designing

30. Many bitmapped images in a sequence is known as

   a) JPEG animation

   b) tweening

   c) TIF animation

   d) GIF animation

31. To convert a file from one type of file to another you can...

   a) Rename the file with a new extension

   b) Use a file conversion program

   c) Both A and B

   d) Open the file and change the file type using the file

32. What kind of animation technique is drawn from frame to frame

   a) Cel animation

   b) Stop Motion

   c) Computer (CGI)

   d) Path animation

33. CGI stands for...

   a) Computer Graphic Images

   b) Computer Generated Imagery

   c) Computer Graphic Interface

   d) None of the above

34. Rotoscoping is a technique when you...

   a) take a series of photos to create movement

   b) use a computer to create a 3D image

   c) trace from a video or film sequence a single frame at a time

   d) move an object a little at a time to create the illusion of movement

35. A technique used in 2D computer graphics that allows animators to see side by side frames at once. That way, the animator can make decisions or edits based on how the previous frames are drawn.

   a) Rendering

   b) Rigging

   c) Onion Skinning

   d) Tweening

36. Leading is:

   a) the amount of white space between each line of type.

   b) drawing a page dummy with a pencil.

   c) what newspaper editors do at staff meetings.

   d) none of the above.

37. Smoothing the edges of shapes, such as letters, on a computer screen is called?

   a) Shaving

   b) Multi-blending

   c) Smudging

   d) Anti-aliasing

38. In typography, kerning means?

   a) To create a scrolling text field.

   b) The spacing between characters on a line of text.

   c) The size of the font.

   d) To rotate the text around an object.

39. The complete assortment of letters, numerals, punctuation marks and other characters of a specific typeface is called a

   a) pica

   b) italic

   c) font

   d) design concept

40. The typeface used in this Practice Test is 'Times New Roman'. This is known as a

    a) serif typeface

    b) sanserif typeface

    c) sans typeface

    d) common typeface

41. What is the meaning of Bandwidth in Network?

    a) Transmission capacity of a communication channels

    b) Connected Computers in the Network

    c) Class of IP used in Network

    d) None of Above

42. DNS is the abbreviation of

    a) Dynamic Name System

    b) Dynamic Network System

    c) Domain Name System

    d) Domain Network Service

43. Computer Network is

    a) Collection of hardware components and computers

    b) Interconnected by communication channels

    c) Sharing of resources and information

    d) All of the Above

44. What does Router do in a network?

   a) Forwards a packet to all outgoing links

   b) Forwards a packet to the next free outgoing link

   c) Determines on which outing link a packet is to be forwarded

   d) Forwards a packet to all outgoing links except the originated link

45. What is the benefit of the Networking?

   a) File Sharing

   b) Easier access to Resources

   c) Easier Backups

   d) All of the Above

46. Which of the following is NOT a consideration for fair use?

   a) Purpose and character of use

   b) Effect of use on the potential market

   c) Amount used

   d) State copyright policy

47. A student wants to use a popular song for a video he is creating for a class assignment. The best advice to give him would be

   a) choose another song

   b) use only 10 seconds of the song

   c) use only a minute of a song

   d) to go ahead and use the whole song

48. When in doubt about copyright law, an educator should

   a) follow district policy

   b) go ahead and use the work

   c) consult an attorney

   d) request permission from the author of a work

49. When is a work considered copyrighted?

   a) As soon as you write the symbol © and the date on it

   b) After you register it with your government's copyright office

   c) As soon as it's printed, written down, recorded, or saved in any digital format

   d) After you register it with your government's copyright office

50. Which one of the four Creative Commons core conditions is always included in a CC license?

   a) Share Alike (SA)

   b) No Derivatives (ND)

   c) Attribution (BY)

   d) Noncommercial (NC)

51. Which of the following factors is most important to consider when assessing the academic achievement of students from culturally and linguistically diverse backgrounds?

   a) the students' prior opportunities to learn

   b) the students' current grade level

   c) the students' report card grades

   d) the students' standardized district test scores

52. Effective way a teacher can increase learning time and, more importantly, student engagement in the classroom.

   a) Maintain a quiet classroom where students can concentrate and work undisturbed.

   b) Provide tangible rewards for work well done, such as free reading time, passes to the library, or extra credit.

   c) Ensure that assignments are interesting, worthwhile, and easy enough to be completed by each learner at his or her current level of understanding.

   d) Demonstrate a commitment to group discussion and cooperative learning.

53. Which of the following are ways of representing 3D objects?

   a) Wire models

   b) Surface models

   c) Solid models

   d) All of the above

54. Basic shapes (spheres - cubes - cylinders) that act as building blocks to create a project.

   a) Primitive Shapes

   b) Transparency

   c) Secondary Shapes

   d) Polygons

55. Software that uses graphics to click on/buttons instead of typed commands.

   a) Animation

   b) GUI (Graphical User Interface)

   c) Linux

   d) WYSIWYG

56. Teachers use formative assessment to improve instructional methods and student feedback throughout the teaching and learning process. What are the formative assessments?

   a) Entrance Exams

   b) Ongoing assessments, reviews, and observations in a classroom.

   c) They are used to evaluate the effectiveness of instructional programs.

   d) Judgments on/of student competency

57. What are summative assessments used to determine?

   a) Instructional methods and student feedback.

   b) If students have mastered specific competencies and to identify instructional areas that need additional attention.

   c) Valid instruction

   d) Ongoing assignments, reviews, and observations.

58. What is the correct formulae for adding 2 cells together?

    a) A1+A2

    b) +A1/A2

    c) =A1+A2

    d) (A1+A2)

59. What is an image that has tints and shades mixed in with only one color (hue)?

    a) Symmetry

    b) CMYK

    c) RGB

    d) Monochromatic

60. What process in 3D that regenerate your final image or animation?

    a) Rigging

    b) Rendering

    c) Rotoscoping

    d) Morphing

61. A student is playing a video game that has a lot of depth and a very realistic appearance. What type of animation is the student enjoying?

    a) 2d Animation

    b) 3D animation

    c) AVI

    d) Vector Animation

62. The students are using an electronic device that requires a different format in which their animated movie was created. They would need to export the animated movie in a native QuickTime format. What file extension should be chosen?

a) SWF

b) MOV

c) .FLA

d) GIF

63. You have created a 3D skeleton with joints that work as a framework, but the character needs to be animated. What method would be used to pose the joints that rotate and move in a kinematic way?

a) Rigging

b) Rendering

c) Morphing

d) Keyframes

64. The ninth-grade student organization wants to design a website for all the ninth-grade students at their school to provide information about all events and news about the grade level. They have come up with a domain name which domain extension should be used?

a) .mil

b) .edu

c) .com

d) .info

65. An action video game where the player is behind the eyes of the game character?

   a) strategy game

   b) fighting game

   c) first person game

   d) puzzle game

66. A student printed a picture of a tree but notice the tree printed blue. What color is missing from the CMYK?

   a) cyan

   b) key

   c) yellow

   d) Magento

67. The class assignment asked the students to conduct an internet search about plants in Texas. Which Boolean search would be best?

   a) Texas plants

   b) Texas AND plants

   c) Texas OR plants

   d) none of the above

68. Which one is consider a data output device?

   a) monitor

   b) digital camera

   c) mouse

   d) keyboard

69. The student newsletter coordinator has noticed an increase in subscribers and no longer can keep up with the paper log. What application would be best?

   a) Word Processor

   b) Project Management

   c) Spreadsheet

   d) Database

70. What memory is volatile and erased when the power is shut off?

   a) ROM

   b) SDRAM

   c) RAM

   d) SDROM

71. The class has an assignment to create a presentation to display at the school's award event. The students have included music in their presentation, without violating the copy rights law, select the two-best answer.

   a) Choose a specific genre

   b) Use acapella only

   c) Create their own music

   d) Get permission or purchase the right to use commercial music

72. What other markup language that works with HTML by displaying how the webpages appear on the browser?

   a) JavaScript

   b) CSS

   c) HTML

   d) Flash

73. What allows controlled access from outside parties to information in secured networks?

   a) Intranet

   b) FTP

   c) Intranet

   d) Extranet

74. Select the most important parts of the student's presentation skill

   a) Content

   b) Knowledge

   c) Effectiveness

   d) All of the above

75. Compressing an image makes the file

   a) quality better

   b) larger

   c) smaller

   d) transparent

76. What is a subtractive color model used in printing?

   a) CMYK

   b) RBG

   c) Hexadecimal

   d) Duplex printing

77. What is the preferred format for photography?

   a) Vector

   b) PNG

   c) GIF

   d) JPEG

78. Who hires key members of the production team, approve locations, set schedules, handle the production budget and scripts?

   a) Director

   b) Producer

   c) Project Manager

   d) Creative Coordinator

79. A low camera angle will make the subject appear bigger. This camera angle gives the viewer a sense of being powerless.

   a) Bird's eye

   b) Extreme Closeup

   c) Frontal view

   d) Worm's Eye

80. What audio editing would be used if the drag and drop feature is utilized?

   a) nonlinear***

   b) linear

   c) clip covering

   d) all of the above

PRACTICE QUESTION ANSWERS

1. D 2. A 3. C 4. A 5. D 6. A 7. C 8. C 9. B 10. A 11. B 12. C

13. B 14. D 15. B 16. D 17. B 18. A 19. B 20. B 21. A 22. B 23. B 24. A

25. C 26. C 27. A 28. D 29. B 30. D 31. C 32. A 33. B 34. C 35. C 36. A

37. D 38. B 39. C 40. A 41. A 42. C 43. D 44. C 45. D 46. D 47. B 48. D

49. C 50. C 51. A 52. C 53. D 54. A 55. B 56. B 57. B 58. C 59. D 60. B

61. B 62. B 63. A 64. D 65. C 66. C 67. B 68. A 69. D 70. C 71. C, D

72. B 73. D 74. D 75. C 76. A 77. D 78. B 79. D 80. A

Bibliography

Synthesizing perspectives on augmented reality and mobile learning
S. M. Land, H. T. Zimmerman TechTrends, vol. 58, no. 1, p. 3, 2014.

Curry, C. (2003). Universal design accessibility for all learners. Educational Leadership, 61 (2). Hendricks, P., Wahl, L., Stull, L., & Duffield, J. (2003, October). From policy to practice: Achieving equitable access to educational technology. Information Technology and Disabilities, 4. Retrieved September 29, 2004, from http://www.rit.edu/%7Eeasi/itd/itdv09n1/hendricks.htm

Tomlinson, C. (2001). How to differentiate instruction in mixed-ability classrooms. Alexandria, VA: ASCD

Using iPad Apps to Improve Communication Skills for Special Education Preschool Students
Maria Gricelda Martínez 2017

Web Content Accessibility Guidelines 1.0. Wendy Chisholm; Gregg Vanderheiden; Ian Jacobs. W3C. 5 May 1999. W3C Recommendation. URL: https://www.w3.org/TR/WAI-WEBCONTENT/

Mossberger, K., Tolbert, C. J., & McNeal, R. S. (2008). Digital citizenship: The internet, society, and participation. Cambridge, Mass: MIT Press.

Hobbs, R., & Moore, D. C. (2013). *Discovering media literacy: Teaching digital media and popular culture in elementary school.*   Thousand Oaks, CA.: Sage.

edWeb: A professional online community for educators. (n.d.). *edWeb*. Retrieved May 28, 2019, from http://home.edweb.net/

Media and Technology Resources for Educators. (n.d.). *Reviews & Age Ratings*. Retrieved May 28, 2019, from https://www.commonsensemedia.org/educators

Teacher Resources. (n.d.). *MediaSmarts*. Retrieved May 29, 2019, from http://mediasmarts.ca/teacher-resources

Acknowledgments

To all the Certified and soon to be Certified Teachers that I have had the opportunity to be mentor, work alongside teaching the youth, I want to say thank you for being the inspiration for the Nitty Gritty Guide.

Also, without the love and support from my family and friends, this book would not exist. You have given me the inspiration to take this journey although, I have failures including taking the TExES Technology Application 242 Exam on the first try you encourage me to keep striving and not to give up and it is so blissful to be in this place now. Thank you to my two sons Anthony & Micah, my other loving family and friends Kenneth, Kim, Marcus, Damien, Carolyn, Frank, Demarcus, Bryant and so many more

I want to give a specific acknowledgement to the Illustrator of this book Brianna Steele of Color-n-Shades company, she took the time and effort to manifest mind capturing graphic art & illustrations.

About the Author

Velma Shaw has worked with children not only in the social service but educational for over 10 years. She currently has developed 3d animations in which they can be viewed on nulucre.com and https://sites.google.com/view/nulucre/home. Her education background consists of completing academics at Richland College in Computer Information Technology, Substitute Teaching and certification as a Google Educator. She currently works with surrounding DFW area school districts as well as, developing games for Google Play and IOS. Her most recent game is ASCEND which is located on Google play. She has been mentored by Professor Carter in multimedia technology and Dr. Hammerslag in A+ Computer Tech & Networking.

Made in the USA
Coppell, TX
06 April 2022

76132145R10074